Soups

Robin Howe is one of the best, and best known, modern writers on cookery and she already has many successes to her credit. She travels regularly with her husband who is head of a news agency in New Delhi; her journeys have taken her from Iran to Polynesia. Wherever she goes she studies the local cuisine at first-hand, with the result that her recipes are both unusual and entirely original.

Other cookery books available in Pan

Mrs Beeton
All About Cookery

Ada Boni
The Talisman Italian Cook Book

Lousene Rousseau Brunner
New Casserole Treasury

Savitri Chowdhary
Indian Cooking

Theodora FitzGibbon
A Taste of Ireland
A Taste of London
A Taste of Scotland
A Taste of Wales
A Taste of the West Country

Dorothy Hall
The Book of Herbs

Rosemary Hume and Muriel Downes
The Cordon Bleu Book of Jams, Preserves and Pickles

Kenneth Lo
Quick and Easy Chinese Cooking

Claire Loewenfeld and Philippa Back
Herbs for Health and Cookery

R. J. Minney (ed.)
The George Bernard Shaw Vegetarian Cook Book

Marguerite Patten
Learning to Cook

Jennie Reekie
Traditional French Cooking

Constance Spry and Rosemary Hume
The Constance Spry Cookery Book

Katie Stewart
The Times Cookery Book

Marika Hanbury Tenison
Eat Well and Be Slim
Deep-Freeze Cookery
Deep-Freeze Sense

with illustrations by Stewart Black

Soups Robin Howe

Pan Books London and Sydney

First published 1967 by The International Wine and
Food Society Limited
This edition published 1976 by Pan Books Ltd,
Cavaye Place, London SW10 9PG

ISBN 030 24808 1
Printed and bound in Great Britain by
Richard Clay (The Chaucer Press) Ltd, Bungay, Suffolk

For Charlotte and Siobhan

Contents

Introduction

A big man can carry a heavy load –
A good soup can carry a dinner.
(Country proverb)

La Soupe has been the name of the evening meal in parts of rural France for hundreds of years. Our word supper is derived from it. Another word in everyday use is restaurant. In France during the sixteenth century a popular soup was called *restaurant* because it was supposed to have restorative properties. A chef who served this particular soup had the word printed above the door of his eating house and gradually the word acquired its present connotation.

According to the French, the word soup comes from the Latin *suppa* and is of the same family as the Dutch word *sopen* and the German *saufen*. Literally, it means 'to swallow'. According to the Sanskrit, the derivation *su* (good) and *po* (to nourish) can be quoted.

However, the word *potage* has a humble origin since it comes simply from the pot into which the meat and vegetables were thrown to make a main dish. The early Egyptians, we are told, did not use soups particularly; certainly there is not much evidence of their being in great demand in the Mesopotamian areas. However, the Roman Apicius gave in his cooking book a good recipe for lentil and haricot bean soup.

There are thick soups, thin and elegant soups, fish soups and simple soups, fruit and wine soups; so much variety, yet for years the British have looked with suspicion upon soups and consumed them almost under protest. This could be a throw-back to the days when a bowl of soup was a meal in itself, a simple, satisfying country dish of meat and vegetables. As people became more 'cultured' and perhaps more selective in what they ate, they began to despise this simple fare. It was peasant's food. They forgot that peasants know pretty well what is good for them.

Then the tide turned again; soups rose in popularity. They returned to the dining room but with rather more elegance, as an appetite stimulator rather than as a main or single course. Now we have come the full circle, for many of us accept the thicker, more filling soups as a meal to be followed by a salad or cheese.

In spite of a plethora of packaged, cubed, dehydrated and short-cut methods of making soups, there are still a lot of people who prefer to eat good home-made soups. In those murky days of winter and autumn there is nothing quite as good as a bowl of steaming hot soup, 'proper' soup as we used to call it. Or, in the rare days of summer's sultry heat, can there be anything more cooling and, at the same time, satisfying than an iced soup, or even a fruit soup? I doubt it.

The French, great soup makers, are credited with an early mention of soups in a treatise written by Guillaume Tirel, known as Taillevent, a master cook to Charles VI of France, about 1370. However, there is a recipe extant given by one of Richard II's chefs for a cabbage soup in 1390 (*see* page 95).

I consulted, as I often do, the *Oxford Dictionary* and I found under soup this discouraging explanation:

1653 . . . 1. A liquid food prepared by boiling, usually consisting of an extract of meat, other vegetables and seasonings.

Well, this is basically true; soup is a liquid food made by cooking slowly, in water, either meat, poultry, fish or vegetables, or a combination of all such items.

Webster's Dictionary (1911) makes soups even more off-putting:

Soup, any material injected into a horse with a view to changing its speed or temperament.

This may have something to do with the Americanism of 'souping up' a car, and probably all of it comes from doping or souping.

The *London Journal* (1854) XIX, 322, states:

By the term soup-shop the speaker meant those convenient houses where burglars and thieves dispose of any silver or gold plate which may fall into their hands. In such establishments the melting-pots are always kept ready.

The *Oxford Dictionary* also quotes a passage, under soup, from Urquhart's Rabelais. 'Then they made ready store of Cardonadoes . . . and good fat soupes of brewis with snippets.' This is dated 1653, reminding me that William Salmon's cooking book, dated 1696, has nothing listed under soup but one under potage – and this soup varies little from stock making of today, except that in its herbs it includes pennyroyal, a herb little used these days, marigold petals (still used in Jersey), violets, currants, hartshorn shavings, as well as the more usual herbs and spices of today. This particular potage, declared Salmon, is very good against consumption or any defect in the lungs or stomach.

So, soup finds itself the neglected child of the kitchen, the Cinderella; and sadly all too many people are happy enough to use the tinned or packaged soups, depending for variety (for basically they all seem to taste the same) on some curious mixing. The stockpot seems such a bugbear – it is easier to reach for the tin-opener. And yet, once the stockpot is started for the day, it keeps on going without even the need to look into the pot.

Soup has been described as being 'to a dinner what a portico is to a house'. But even a portico, these days, is outdated. Soup is not only the beginning of a meal but it should also announce the full tone of the dinner, 'as an overture of an opera announces the subject of the work'.

In other words, soups must be in harmony with the rest of the meal. It is no wonder that many gourmets consider soup making to be the ultimate accomplishment of the chef. 'Soup, you know, is not to be entrusted to just anyone. It is the job for the expert cook. In big hotels, to be the master of the soup is a high office, next to that of the sauce chef himself', is the advice of a chef.

Much of the culinary wisdom of the East has been deployed in the making of soups. We are told that Confucius left his wife because she was not a good cook. Even I would have thought this was somewhat arbitrary treatment. In our times, P. Morton Shand, a man of decided culinary views, wrote that to possess a cook who makes the perfect soup is to possess a jewel of great price. In France, where soup is still the basis of national diet, with centuries of experience, Brillat-Savarin, in the nineteenth century, claimed that the French had brought the art of soup making to a pitch 'which can only be called perfection'.

Mr Shand felt deeply about soup. 'A woman who cannot make soup should not be allowed to marry', he pleaded; and 'There ought to be a Chair of Soup Making in Newnham and "blues" (or rather Cordons Bleus) should be awarded to rival teams of broth makers. A pass "plate" in soups should be made compulsory for every woman in every faculty, while the degree of Domina Jurie Facimundae d'Ecrevisses might well be the honours diploma theme.' All of this, he felt, would enhance the marriage prospects of women undergraduates which, he added peevishly, are otherwise poor in the extreme.

So there we are. Mr Shand knew what he was talking about, although he had some harsh things to say about some of the world's famous soups. He insisted that the Germans simply cannot make soups – but felt that the Russian bortsch 'is a source of pure gastronomic joy'. 'I have been told,' he adds, 'that the choicest varieties of the vast bortsch family require forty-eight hours of preparation by an army of scullery wenches.' But gravy soup shall be passed over in compassionate silence, as 'Switzerland's best-known soup'. (I disagree with him.)

I am not happy about the many wine and beer soups, but I know they are popular in their countries of origin, also with many tourists and gourmets.

Some people feel that fruit soups, while delicious in themselves, are not soups. But what else are they? Our Christmas pudding started life as porridge.

Soup through the ages has played a role similar to bread. As a basic food every country, every civilization, has had its soup. France its *pot-au-feu*, Italy its minestrone, Russia its bortsch, China its birds' nest soup, etc. Soups have been celebrated in literature from the beginning of time.

There is the Biblical reference to Jacob's pottage: did not Esau sell his birthright for this mess of pottage which, we are told, is our favourite lentil soup? Esau surely must be claimed as the first declared gastronome, his partiality for soup being such that he was willing to make this sacrifice. Lewis Carroll's *Soup of the Evening, Beautiful Soup* is one of his most quoted lines. Soup has inspired positively lyrical descriptions. 'There is nothing like a plate of hot soup, its wisp of aromatic steam making the nostrils quiver with anticipation', wrote the ecstatic Louis P. de Gouy in 1949.

Queen Elizabeth I and Queen Victoria, we are told, were fond of sipping a bowl of mutton broth at breakfast; it woke up their appetites. Breakfast soups were popular with such famous people as Ignace Paderewski and Leopold Stokowski. Drunks also find a breakfast soup better even than a prairie oyster. The Italian composer Giuseppe Verdi gracefully attributed much of his inspiration to the warming and sustaining effects of a large bowl of soup.

Since time immemorial country people the world over have kept the stockpot simmering all day long on the kitchen stove. I doubt whether it was kept on longer than the day's cooking, since the contents of the stockpot were meant for eating. During periods of disaster and stress, soup kitchens have served as an excellent method of feeding large masses of hungry people.

'The proper stimulant with which to start a dinner', said Dr Leipold, an eminent dietician, 'is a hot plate of good soup, not a cocktail or hors d'oeuvre.' And there is no doubt that an otherwise impeccable dinner can be ruined by a poor soup. The soup, if good, takes the edge off the appetite and, if the next course is not quite up to standard, the diner might not be so critical – he has enjoyed the first course: it has lifted his appetite, warmed his heart and given the meal a fine start, as all soups should do. 'Soups challenge us, because an enticing, flavourful soup can be as different from the thin, watery beverage erroneously called soup, as the genuine green turtle is from mock turtle soup,' wrote Louis de Gouy. He is right.

Soups can be divided broadly into two classes, clear and thick. Thick soup can be divided into those which are not puréed or creamed, and those which are. Clear soups can be hot or cold, liquid or jellied. Both clear and jellied soups give a cachet to a formal dinner; thick soups are intended more for lunches and for serving as a main course.

The line between soups and broths is hard to define. Many soups are as thick as a ragoût. Our boiled beef started in the stockpot. Soups and stews have gone hand in hand in the world's cuisine, and their origins are lost in antiquity. When the subject is explored, a curious relationship between soups and puddings emerges.

One of the earliest references to English soups is: 'It is a kind of sweet, pleasant broth, made rich with fruit or vegetables and spices.' These popular sweetened soups became thicker as the years passed and thus our bread and rice puddings evolved.

Finally, many soups are low in calorie value. The bean and pea soups, with a high percentage of the human dietary requirements, are a good source of one or more nutritional factors of importance. Soups, because of their nutritive value, should play an important part in the diet of children, invalids and older people.

All in all, the more one considers the pleasures and the value of soup and all its side issues, the more one is surprised that soup is not on the table of every Englishman, as it is of every Frenchman.

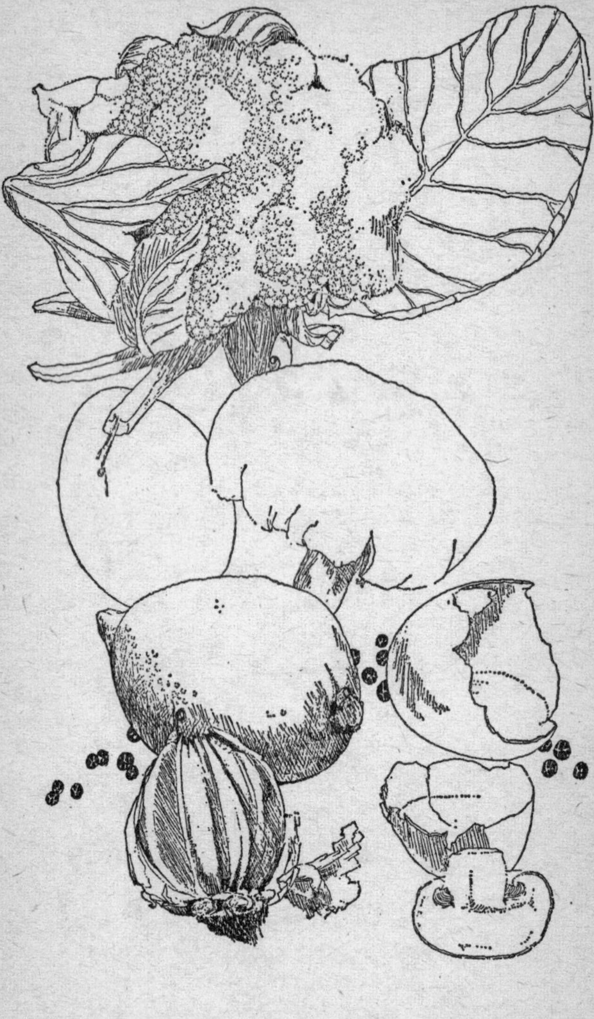

General instructions

Service and presentation

Usually soups are served after the hors d'oeuvre, if offering both, but the general practice is to serve hors d'oeuvre at noon and soup at dinner. Consommé and all clear soups are best served in soup bowls or two-handled soup cups. The quantity held is much the same as the conventional soup plate but the appearance and, curiously, the flavour are different, although I am prepared to believe that this is my imagination.

Thick soups can be served in bowls or plates; I prefer to serve vegetable soups in plates, although many people use bowls for these as well.

Jellied soups can, I think, only be served in cups, although I have met Americans who served them in glass or crystal bowls. Actually, some of the deeper, old-fashioned finger bowls are rather fun for a really good amber-coloured jellied soup.

Some soups really demand a soup tureen and these lovely bits of Victoriana (and earlier) are again coming into their own. I think it is rather nice to serve soup from a tureen and, in any case, in servantless days rather more simple than struggling to and fro with bowls or plates. Once I served a splendid Chinese soup in a winter melon standing in a Celadon jardinière. I was terrified that the jardinière might be broken but all went well. And the dinner, simply because of its impressively served soup, was a huge success.

The choice of soup is important, depending entirely upon the occasion. Clear soup and consommé should precede a dinner of several courses, its purpose being to put the diners in the right mood. As Grimod de la Reynière so wisely said, 'reflecting the wealth to follow, in a way that an overture announces the main theme of the *Opéra Comique*'.

Thick soups, on the other hand, are no overture, they are the theme; basically good hearty peasant soups, served as a main course, with no nonsense, in good deep plates or peasant bowls.

Delicate soups, suggests one culinary expert of earlier times, should be left for ladies' luncheons. I so seldom have such luncheons that I cannot endorse or deny this rather Cranfordian line of thinking.

Unusual soups are for the brave and the experimentalists. But the serving of them is normal, except those fruit soups which can be served either before or after the meal. With Chinese food, why not emulate the Chinese and try a soup half-way through the meal?

Recipes and their use

It is important to remember that no recipe, except those which are absolutely basic, should be considered unalterable. I always feel that a recipe should first be tried out as it is given; if it pleases, continue thus: if not, make changes, vary it at will; you may improve upon it. The varying of recipes is an amusing art of cooking and an infinite variety can be evolved by a judicious admixture of flavours and seasonings. As one culinary writer so nicely expressed it: 'Every recipe is waiting expectantly to be improved upon; this immortal genius might be you'.

I have lived in many and various parts of the world and have had to learn to condition my recipes according to the ingredients to hand. One of our West Indian subterfuges was to cook a small, pale green gourd with the juice of several limes to produce a passable imitation of stewed apples. The flavour was not at all bad. Not, of course, as good as the real thing but sufficiently so to evoke memories.

In the same way with the following recipes. If a particular ingredient is difficult to obtain, try its nearest cousin. There is usually a near relative. Of course, if the recipe calls for an ingredient which is absolutely impossible to obtain, then there is nothing for it but to abandon the idea – but not before all ingenuity has been exhausted and all avenues of enquiry explored. Nowadays in the big cities it is surprising what a little good detective work can unearth.

Bread slices

Bread for dropping into soups should not be sliced anyhow. If it is, it remains stodgy, as unappetizing to the palate as to the eye. The correct manner in which to slice bread for soup is to slice off a good square piece of bread, free from crust, and then cut off the corner on the slant, diagonally, and slice it thus in parallel lines, just as you would cut cloth, on the cross. Thus cut, the bread appears to disintegrate easily into the soup and blends pleasantly, without its presence being too obvious.

Cream

In many of the following recipes, fresh cream is called for and often sour cream. Both of these are easily obtainable, the first from all dairies and delicatessen stores, the latter from supermarkets, also from delicatessen stores, especially those dealing with Polish and Jewish foods. From time to time, however, a recipe calls for scalded cream, and this has a flavour which is entirely different from fresh cream. The cream, which must be fresh, should be allowed to reduce quite considerably by boiling. It can then be added to any soup without fear of curdling.

Liaison

This is a term for the agent used to bind ingredients together, as, for example, an egg binds meat together to make forcemeat. In soups it is simply a culinary process designed to give body to liquid food, to sauces, broths or soups. This can be done either with flour or with eggs.

When adding eggs or cream to soups, care must be taken to avoid curdling. Eggs are always added with the pan off the heat, immediately before serving, and the soup on no account should be allowed to boil after the eggs have been added. Equal care applies to the adding of fresh cream. The soup may be simply reheated with immense care and much stirring.

Again, when adding flour or cornflour, care must be observed to avoid ugly, ill-flavoured lumps. Both are added at least fifteen minutes before the soup is ready. It is important that the flour is properly cooked, otherwise there is the odour and flavour of uncooked flour. Some people thicken their soups and sauces with a flour and water paste, but it is far better to make a roux (*see* below).

Roux

This is a mixture of butter or other fatty substance and flour, cooked together for varying periods: how long depends upon the ultimate use. It is a thickening element in soups and even more so in sauces.

There are basically three kinds of roux; white, blond and brown. If too much roux is made, or if it is easier to make a batch of roux, it will keep a fair time.

A roux is made by heating butter (or other fat) and adding, usually, an equal quantity of flour. This is done gradually and the mixture is stirred all the while. A white roux is made in some five minutes, a blond one takes somewhat longer, while the brown roux takes up to ten minutes. Stirring should be done with a wooden spoon.

It is the amount of butter which determines the thickness of the roux. If a thin liquid is required, use two parts of butter to one of flour. When dripping is used, it is generally better to use rather more flour than fat.

Soup which has been added to a roux (and soup must always be added to the roux, never the other way round) must be allowed to simmer for at least fifteen minutes to get rid of the uncooked flour odour.

Cornflour can be made into a thin paste to be added to piping hot soup and stirred carefully and briskly. Indeed, some of the recipes in this book call for cornflour. In Chinese cooking, cornflour is a favourite ingredient.

Salt

That important pinch of salt. 'That precious salt, that gold of cookery'. The discovery of salt was one of the earliest and most important developments of culinary arts. Since time immemorial it has been an important item of man's diet and nutrition and over the centuries has become the most important seasoning in the world. There is hardly a dish which is not improved by 'a pinch of salt'.

There should be four types of salt in the well-equipped kitchen, table, rock, kitchen and celery.

Pepper

The spiciest of all spices is pepper. And what we call pepper is not related to sweet pepper or capsicum. Pepper grows in a tropical plant or vine bearing spike-shaped clusters of fruit which contain the round peppercorns. As a condiment, it is second only to salt, its twin. It is used all over the world and on practically every table. Food without pepper would be sad.

Like its brother spices, pepper has had its romance. It came originally from the Malabar coast of India, but today most of it comes from what used to be known as the Dutch East Indies, Indonesia. Sarawak also is one of the main producers. The Greeks were using pepper as early as the fourth century BC, but in those days only the rich could afford it since it had to be transported half-way across the world to reach those ancient Greek tables – and the route was wild and dangerous.

Unlike salt, pepper is not essential to health, although it is good for the disposition. Taxes and tribute have been paid with pepper.

Black pepper is much stronger than white pepper and is made

by drying the peppers or berries until they are black. White pepper is made by grinding the seeds as they are taken from the berry.

To get the best out of pepper, buy a pepper mill and grind it yourself. There are several kinds of pepper mills on the market and, for those with patience and a feeling for flavour, I do recommend using one. Pepper has a tendency to lose its pungency soon after being ground, so that freshly ground pepper adds more flavour to cooking, and an extra thrill.

Cayenne pepper is a member of the paprika or capsicum family and not related to true pepper.

Bouquet garni (a bunch of herbs)

This consists of a combination of parsley, thyme and bay leaf and is much used in soups, stews and braised meats or ragoûts. The bunches can be large, medium or small. If the herbs are fresh, and they are much nicer when fresh, they are all wrapped inside the parsley and tied together with cotton or fine string. For special dishes, other herbs are added but then the recipe usually specifies it. Thus a bouquet garni with fennel, or sweet marjoram.

A bouquet garni is always removed before serving. Dried herbs, to be made into a bouquet garni, are wrapped in fine muslin and it is possible to buy them already prepared for dropping into the soup, etc.

Garlic

Do not fear garlic It has a long and famous history. The Romans believed it had magical powers, and the ancient Greeks detested it. They have had a change of taste since. At one time it was despised by the British, but these days it is pretty generally accepted by the rising generation of people interested in cooking.

There is nothing subtle about garlic. Its flavour cannot be described as fleeting. Although some cooks declare that chewing a sprig of fresh parsley will take away its aftermath, the true garlic eater knows that nothing but time succeeds in removing its odour.

By and large garlic should be used sparingly and it is not generally necessary to cut it. Far better to make an incision in the clove, after peeling, and remove it before serving.

As a flavouring, no one should be able to say definitely that garlic has been used (unless the dish is meant to taste of garlic, which is another matter); on the other hand, its flavour should be missed if lacking.

When taking off the cloves of garlic do so without breaking them. Once the clove is broken or cut, some of its oil escapes. It is advisable to have a special chopping board both for garlic and for onions; also to use a stainless steel knife since the escaping oil does often stain. To remove the odour and possible stain from hands, board and knife, wash all in warm, soapy water.

Spices

Throughout history man has prized spices highly and regarded them as a luxury. How many of us when we see neat little rows of kitchen spices realize that spice has a violent and romantic history? At times the survival of nations hung virtually on a bagful of spices. One of the earliest civilizations, the Babylonians, are known to have grown spices in their lovely gardens; they played an important part in that country's economy.

Spices are coming back into the British kitchen, not only the everyday ones which we all know but some of the more exotic. It is true they now come ground in jars, but it is a beginning. It is so much better to buy spices whole and to grind them oneself. There are several gadgets on the market which assist this operation, which is not as tiresome as one might imagine. However, if one must buy spices ground, and better this way than not at all, then do buy in small quantities. Spices lose their fragrance and taste so quickly.

Among the most usual spices are cloves and coriander seeds;

the latter is the spicy seed of a small plant belonging to the parsley family which is dried for seasoning. It is much used in Oriental cooking. Then cumin, another member of the parsley family that is native to the Middle East. It has a somewhat bitter taste but is much used as a condiment. In Europe it is often used to flavour soups. Caraway seeds, the fruit of a biennial plant grown in northern and central Europe, are much used in soups and stews in central Europe, less in cakes as formerly in Britain. The plant has pleasant white or pinkish flowers and the seeds are very agreeable.

Then cinnamon, one of the most aromatic and oldest of our spices. It is mentioned in the Old Testament as used in incense. And it is recorded that women in the Orient used it to perfume their beds. Cinnamon proper is the prepared bark of a tree which is related to the laurel. It is possible to buy cinnamon in sticks and in this way you will obtain a true cinnamon flavour. It must be broken into 2·5-cm (inch-sized) pieces when using.

Ginger: for the recipes in this book, green or raw ginger is required. Ginger has one of the loveliest flowers with a sweet perfume. It grows easily in Jamaica, China and in parts of India. It is the root which we eat and this grows into a palm-shape with fingers. For this it has been styled 'a hand'.

There is mace with its delicate flavour and pretty lacy appearance. Mace forms an aril round the nutmeg, hence the similarity in their flavours. However, the two are different and used in different ways. Mace when fresh is red, but fades when dried for commercial use. Nutmeg, one of the most used of spices, should be bought whole. Nutmeg graters are easily available and there is a wealth of difference in the flavour between the freshly ground and commercially prepared.

Paprika, a red powdery spice, is obtained by grinding the ripe, dried fruit of the capsicum. I prefer to use only the genuine Hungarian sweet paprika in my cooking for this has a rich flavour and enhances the flavour of the food, especially a good, rich meat soup.

Saffron, an essential in Oriental cooking, requires soaking in water before using. It is the stigmas of a special purple crocus; it grows in Spain, also in Kashmir. A Kashmiri hardly considers his food as food if not flavoured with saffron.

Finally chillies and Cayenne pepper, which I have referred to in the pepper notes. Both are members of the capsicum family.

Freezing

Almost all soups, and certainly all stocks, will freeze extremely well. I have kept soup and stock for weeks at a time. They ice up but thaw easily, and when I want only half of the iced soup, I simply go to it with an ice pick. If the soup is frozen as soon as it is cool then it retains its flavour. Even fish soups freeze.

The soup or stock should be packed into freezing containers and about 2·5cm (one inch) headroom allowed. If you are freezing soups which will require milk or cream, these two ingredients should not be added until the soups are to be served. Potatoes are also better left out of soups for freezing.

When ready to use the soup or stock, either thaw it slowly at room temperature or, if in a hurry, hold the container over running hot water to loosen the soup, which is a lump of ice. Then turn it into a saucepan and cook it slowly until it is reheated. You can then deal with it as you do with freshly made soup or stock.

I usually freeze a couple of pints of soup or stock at a time. In America stock is often frozen in ice-cube pans and the individual cubes of ice then wrapped in paper and left until required in the deep-freeze.

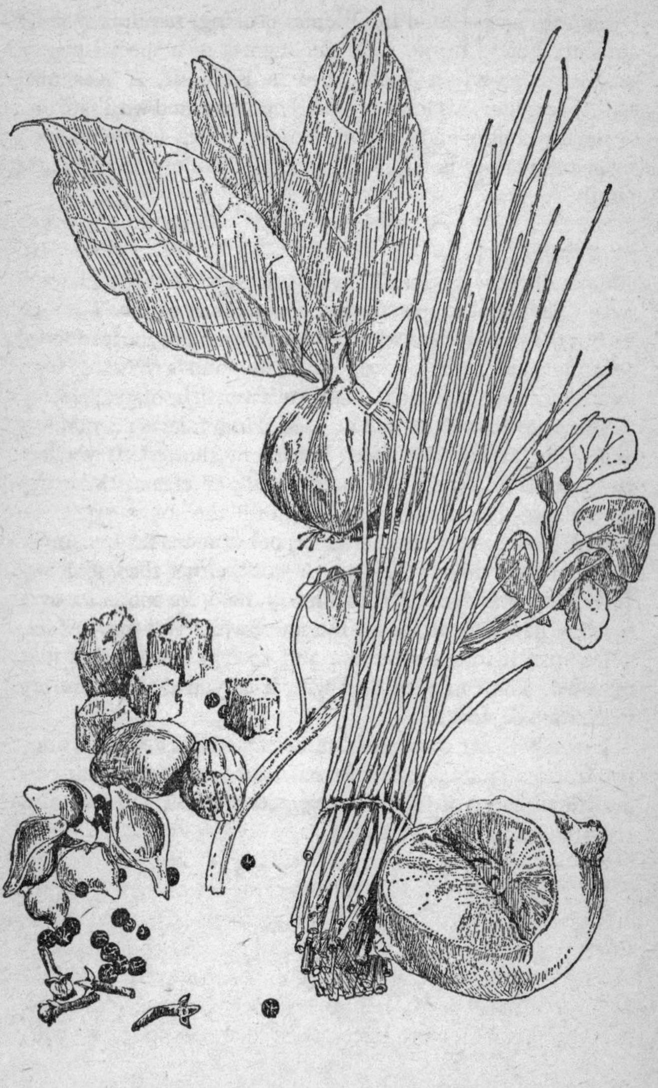

Garnishing

A garnish is the technical name for any additions made to the soup just before serving. It is perfectly simple to produce an endless variety of soups just by changing the garnishes.

Not all soups need garnishing, or dressing up, but most of them are much improved both in appearance and flavour by doing so. Sprigs of parsley, chopped chives, chervil, rosemary, strips of celery or lettuce; golden-brown, crisp croûtons, all these will go a long way towards stimulating appetites as well as changing the flavour of soups which, whether crystal clear or thick and creamy, are a perfect foil for almost all herbs and spices.

Bean soups, fish soups and even a consommé are much improved by savory, a herb of the mint family which used to be known as the bean herb for obvious reasons. Finely-chopped watercress or its young, tender leaves, used whole, give colour and flavour to white creamed soups. Caraway seeds add distinction to cauliflower soups, as well as character to a goulash.

Those who like curry powder, and can make a good one not over-flavoured with turmeric, will find it adds something to pea soups, while chilli powder helps corn soups. Unusual and not often used in Britain are poppy seeds which, after being lightly toasted, are splendid served with a cream of chicken soup. So are sesame seeds sprinkled on hot buttered cracker biscuits and offered with one-course meals. Chopped dill is almost essential to a beetroot soup, so is finely-chopped mint to a plain carrot soup. Spinach soup benefits by the addition of grated nutmeg, as well as by finely-chopped rosemary or chives, and lemon juice. Basil marries perfectly with tomato soups; fish soup cries out for chopped basil, dill or fennel.

Chopped blanched almonds are to be recommended with creamed chicken soup. Salted whipped cream, or sour cream, when used as a garnish, can be tinted with paprika, saffron or vegetable colouring for added flavour and elegance. Thin rounds of frankfurters are excellent with lentil or split pea soups, and pastry sticks generously sprinkled with caraway seeds can be served with many soups.

Other good garnishes (apart from those immediately following) can be obtained by the use of hard-boiled eggs, finely-chopped cooked vegetables and pastas (especially tiny ravioli). Pasta and rice should, if a clear soup is demanded, be cooked separately and then dropped into the soup, to prevent clouding.

Grated Parmesan or other hard cheese is acceptable in a large number of soups, and a few drops of Tabasco help a consommé. Far better still is Jamaican pepper wine. This is made by steeping small hot chilli peppers in sherry and leaving for three months before using. It is very hot, only a few drops need be added and it is heavenly in any clear soup. (I have had made for a small liqueur bottle a silver top just like the top of an Angostura bottle which shakes out just the right quantity when it is used.) It keeps a very long time indeed.

Finally, wines must be considered, but here both care and restraint must be exercised. Soup, whatever its garnish, should taste of the substance from which it takes its name. The best wines for flavouring, unless otherwise specified, are Madeira, Marsala or sherry, and generally fruity rather than dry. One dessertspoonful should be enough for four people. Bad or stale wine is not going to do anything for a soup, and cheap, so-called cooking sherry even less. The same applies to too much seasoning, or too heavy a hand with flavouring or seasoning sauces. These latter were thought to 'bring out the flavour' of soups, but all they succeed in doing is to give their own flavour to any soup they touch.

Chiffonnade

This can be composed of one or more vegetables, such as lettuce, spinach or sorrel, but not of the pod varieties, i.e. peas or beans. Cut the leaves into match-like strips, drop them into iced, salted water to become crisp, then blanch in fish or meat stock until they are barely tender. Float these strips in each plate or bowl of soup. To keep its aroma and character, the chiffonnade should not be added to the soup until the very last moment.

A chiffonade may be used for either thick or clear soups, and only a little may be used in each serving.

Croûtons

These are small cubes or squares of bread which have been browned by frying or baking. They can be made in advance, stored in a closed tin and kept in a cool, dry place for at least two weeks.

1 Cut a slice of bread as for toast and remove the crusts. Cut into fingers, then into small squares or cubes – not too small or they become like small shot when cooked. Have ready a pan with a little melted, smoking-hot butter. Fry the cubes quickly until crisp and a golden brown.

Toasted bread, however crisp, does not make a substitute for fried or baked croûtons. As soon as the pieces meet the soup they swell and disintegrate.

2 Cut croûtons as above, dip quickly in and out of milk. Roll in grated dry cheese, place on a greased baking-sheet in a single layer and bake in a very hot oven until the cheese is melted and the bread crisp.

3 Cut the bread as above, place on an ungreased baking-sheet and grill under a good flame until crisp.

4 Cut the bread as above, dip into a seasoning (to choice) and brown in a hot oven, or under a hot grill until crisp.

5 Cut the bread as above, dip into well-beaten egg, then fry until crisp in smoking-hot fat.

6 Cut the bread as above, but fry the cubes in garlic-flavoured fat.
7 Cut the bread as above, dip into stock from which the fat has not yet been removed. Drop the cubes on to a greased baking sheet, brown in a hot oven till crisp and a delicate golden-brown colour.

Crumbled bacon
Fry or grill bacon till very crisp, cook and crumble. Sprinkle on vegetable soups and even some fish soups, in particular cream of haddock.

Diablotins
Beat 2 or 3 egg yolks. Add sufficient grated Gruyère and Parmesan cheese mixed to make a thick paste. Season generously with salt, cayenne pepper and paprika. Cut small rounds of bread, preferably French, and spread each piece 5 mm (¼″) thick with the sauce, forming little domes of cheese in the centre. Brown in a very quick oven for a few minutes and serve with the soup; or drop into a consommé immediately before serving.

Instead of egg yolks, a very thick béchamel sauce may be used.

Also called diablotins are small cheese-flavoured *profiteroles* (*see* page 36), and chocolates sold in paper cases accompanied by a motto.

Dough peas (Austria)

3 tablespoonfuls flour
1·5 dl (¼ pint) milk
1 beaten egg
salt, pepper
grated cheese to taste

Mix 3 tablespoonfuls flour with the milk. Add salt and pepper (rather generously), and grated cheese to taste. Beat well, then add 1 thoroughly-beaten egg. Have ready in a pan enough smoking-hot fat or oil to cover the peas. Pour the batter through a wire sieve: it will flow very quickly and easily without pushing. Let the batter fry to a light brown. Drain well and serve hot or cold. The little dough peas separate without trouble. They can be offered separately or in the soup. They are delicious, make a change from croûtons, and are just as easy to prepare.

Instead of cheese one may add tomato purée or ketchup or any type of flavouring liked, but with less milk. Dried herbs can also be used as a flavouring and, if using dough peas with fish soup, anchovy ketchup rings a change in flavour.

Cheese and chives dumplings

1 stiffly-beaten egg white
1½ tablespoonfuls flour
pinch salt, pepper and nutmeg
dash Tabasco, or chilli sauce
2 tablespoonfuls each grated cheese and chopped chives

Fold the flour into the white of egg, beat again and add the salt, pepper, nutmeg and sauce. Blend well and add the cheese and chives. Drop by teaspoonfuls into the hot soup, cover the pan, lower the heat and simmer for 3–4 minutes.

Meat dumplings (Denmark)

325 gr (¾ lb) finely-minced beef
50 gr (2 oz) finely-grated suet
1 heaped tablespoonful flour
2 eggs
salt, pepper and grated onion to taste
1·5 dl (¼ pint) cream

Mix the beef and suet, add the flour, eggs, pepper, salt and onion. Pound this in a mortar, or put it through a mincer again. Knead until it becomes like a tough batter. Stir in the cream, a little at a time, then shape the mixture into small dumplings. To test whether the texture is correct, boil one. If it holds up (and it should) and does not break, all is well. If not, add a little more flour. Drop the dumplings into boiling, clear soup and cook for about 15 minutes.

These little dumplings are extremely smooth, almost rubbery, but light and good. The above quantity makes about 36 small dumplings and they can be deep frozen if this is too much. But, as they are small, six to eight can be given in one serving. For chicken dumplings, substitute chicken for meat.

Semolina dumplings (Germany and Hungary)

1·5 dl (¼ pint) mixed milk and water
25 gr (1 oz) butter
½ teaspoonful sugar
75 gr (3 oz) semolina
2 eggs (1 if very large)
salt, pinch of nutmeg

Bring the milk and water to the boil with the sugar, salt and nutmeg. Sprinkle in the semolina – do this with some care, otherwise it becomes lumpy and is difficult to smooth. Stir the mixture over a low heat until it comes away cleanly from the saucepan. Leave the mixture to cool a little, then add 1 egg; when this is thoroughly blended into the mixture add, if necessary, the remaining egg. Break off pieces, shape into balls and poach in boiling water or in the boiling soup. The dumplings are very light and are ready when they rise to the top.

Snow dumplings (Germany)

Beat 2 egg whites until stiff and gradually fold in 50 gr (2 oz) caster sugar. Pour this mixture into a pan three-quarters filled with boiling water. Cover the pan, then draw it to the side of the stove. Leave for 15 minutes. When the mixture has swollen, cut it into dumpling-sized pieces. Remove these with a draining spoon and serve at once.

Very useful for fruit soups, but in Germany these dumplings are often served with beer and wine soup.

Egg balls

Press 4 hard-boiled egg yolks through a fine sieve. Add salt and pepper, a dash of nutmeg and enough slightly-beaten egg white to moisten the mixture. Shape into balls, roll these in flour and fry in hot butter until the balls are a golden-brown.

Various flavourings may also be used, such as saffron, anchovy essence, tomato or mushroom ketchup, Worcester sauce, curry powder or chilli sauce.

Egg yolks can be boiled quite easily without their whites. Simply drop them into boiling, slightly salted water, as when poaching whole eggs.

Buttered eggs

Thoroughly beat 2 or 3 eggs, add salt and pepper, a little grated onion or finely-chopped chives. Heat 25 gr (1 oz) butter in a small saucepan, add the eggs, cook quickly (scramble or butter) but let the mixture become quite firm, almost hard. Chop to serve in soups.

Egg rain (China)

Beat 1 or 2 eggs into 3 dl (½ pint) milk or cream, or a mixture of both. Add salt and pepper and whisk this into the soup while it is still boiling. Continue to boil for 1 minute only.

Egg and garlic sauce (Turkey)

4 cloves garlic
1 teaspoonful salt
2 egg yolks
olive oil
lemon juice, or wine vinegar

Pound the garlic with the salt to a pulp, beat in the yolks, then gradually add, drop by drop, enough olive oil to make a sauce of mayonnaise consistency. Loosen with the lemon juice or vinegar. Add to the soup just before serving, like the *pistou* (*see* page 111).

Egg and lemon sauce

This is an exceedingly popular Greek, Turkish and Balkan favourite.

4 egg yolks
4 tablespoonfuls strained lemon juice
2–3 tablespoonfuls hot broth

Beat the yolks till light, then slowly add the juice, beating all the while. Gradually add the broth (from the soup), mix well, then stir back into the soup. Leave for 5 minutes on the side of the stove. Above all, do not let the soup boil again, and keep the pan covered.

Egg and sherry sauce

2 beaten eggs
1 tablespoonful sherry (medium dry)
2 tablespoonfuls hot broth

Stir the sherry into the beaten eggs, add the broth, return this to the soup and serve at once.

Fluffy pancakes for garnishing (Switzerland)

100 gr (4 oz) flour
2 egg whites
2 egg yolks
about 2 dl (6 fl. oz) milk
oil or butter for frying
finely-chopped chives
good pinch salt

Sift the flour and salt into a basin and beat in the egg yolks, one at a time. Let this rest for 15 minutes. Gradually beat in the milk. Beat the whites till stiff and fold these into the batter. Lightly grease a frying pan and drop in 1 tablespoonful of the batter. Let it spread very thinly. Fry on one side for 2 or 3 minutes, or till properly cooked. Turn out of the pan. Repeat this till all the batter is used up. Cut the pancakes into thin strips, like noodles, and drop these into boiling consommé or very clear stock. Add grated chives. These pancakes are best made immediately before using, otherwise they become tough.

Frimsells (Switzerland)

Lightly beat 2 eggs, adding a little salt, then add as much flour to them as they will absorb to make a dough sufficiently firm to roll out thin as a wafer. Dust this lightly with flour and roll into a 'Swiss' roll. Cut this into the thinnest possible of strips, i.e. spaghetti-size, and shake out the strips. Drop these into boiling soup; it should be at a rolling boil. Cook them for 15–20 minutes.

Herb toasts

Chop very fine, in equal proportions, chervil, parsley, tarragon and chives. Mix these with about 100 gr (4 oz) soft fresh butter. Add salt and pepper to taste and a little pounded garlic. Spread this mixture on thin slices of French bread (other types of white bread can also be used) and toast the slices in a moderate oven till a golden-brown and crisp.

These can be added to bowls of soup at the very last moment, but they will naturally swell. They may also be served as a side dish to be eaten with the soup.

Omelette (Romania)

This garnish can be used with any clear stock or consommé.

6 servings

2 egg whites
2 egg yolks
1½ teaspoonfuls flour
salt, pepper
½ teaspoonful grated lemon rind
½ teaspoonful finely-chopped dill or tarragon

Beat the egg whites till stiff. Beat the yolks till smooth, add the flour and continue beating till this mixture is blended smoothly. Add salt and pepper to taste, the lemon rind and herbs. Fold in the whites. When the soup is boiling (and this should be just before it is to be used), pour the egg mixture over the top. It will form a blanket or omelette. Cover the pan and cook for 3 minutes – over a very low heat it can cook for a few minutes longer. As you pour the soup into bowls, break off pieces of the omelette to garnish each bowl.

Plain pancake

Prepare the pancake mixture using any favourite method. The batter should be flavoured generously with salt and pepper, with cheese, or grated and pounded onion, tomato, mushroom or anchovy ketchup. Fry the pancakes in the usual manner but make them thicker than usual. Take them from the pan, roll and cut into very thin strips and drop these into bowls or plates of clear hot soup.

Profiteroles for soup (France)

1·5 dl (¼ pint) cold water
50 gr (2 oz) butter
½ teaspoonful salt
pinch pepper
dash nutmeg (optional)
65 gr (2½ oz) flour
2 small eggs

Bring the water with the butter to the boil and cook slowly till the butter has melted. Add, all at once, the flour, salt, pepper and nutmeg. Beat vigorously for a few seconds to blend thoroughly, then work the dough over a moderately high heat till it forms a ball, leaves the side of the pan and begins to film up the bottom.

Take the pan from the fire and turn the dough on to a board. Let it cool. Make a well in the centre and break an egg into the middle of the well. Beat it into the dough till it is absorbed, then add the remaining egg. Beat till the dough is smooth. Fill a pastry bag with this mixture and press tiny balls on to the floured baking sheet. Bake the puffs in a slow oven till well risen and crisp, about 10 minutes with these tiny ones. Turn off the heat, prick each puff and return them to the oven (without heat) and leave the door ajar. Let them cool before using. They can be fried in deep hot fat, or the dough may be wrapped round tiny pieces of Gruyère cheese before cooking.

In old-time French cooking, *profiteroles* were nothing more than small pieces of bread. Now these pieces of bread have been changed into the more delicate, though not always so simple to make, choux pastry puffs which should be the size of a very small nut. These tiny puffs take only a matter of minutes to cook in a hot oven and, as soon as they are taken from the oven when they are firm and dry to the touch, they should be punctured to release the steam. If left, they will become soggy, as the centre part, even in the tiny shells, is uncooked and its dampness will spread.

Quenelles

These three recipes will each produce about 40 small *quenelles*.

Bread quenelles (Germany)

175 gr (7 oz) soft breadcrumbs
75 gr (3 oz) butter
1·5 dl (¼ pint) cream
2–3 egg yolks
salt and pepper
grated Parmesan cheese, about 1 tablespoonful

Melt the butter, work in the breadcrumbs, moisten this with the cream and knead to a smooth paste. When cool, add the egg yolks, salt, pepper and Parmesan cheese. Shape into *quenelles*, or dumplings. Test one in boiling water to see that it is of the correct consistency; if so, poach them all, or fry in deep boiling fat.

If frying these *quenelles*, they should be served separately. If the paste should prove too thick, add a little more cream; if too thin, a little flour.

Chicken quenelles

100 gr (4 oz) minced, uncooked chicken, veal or game
50 gr (2 oz) very thick béchamel sauce
salt and pepper

Pound the meat to a paste, mix it into the sauce, add salt and pepper to taste and break off pieces; a floured hand is required for these *quenelles* as they are sticky. Shape into balls and drop into boiling stock; or they can be fried in hot butter or olive oil.

Fish quenelles

100 gr (4 oz) minced cooked fish (tinned shellfish or salmon may be used)
50 gr (2 oz) soft white breadcrumbs
25 gr (1 oz) melted butter
little chopped parsley or other green herbs
salt and pepper
2 egg yolks, lightly beaten

Mix all these ingredients together, break off small pieces, shape into balls and cook for 10 minutes in boiling fish stock or soup. They are particularly good when made with crabmeat.

Royale (Egg Custard)

This garnish for soups is prepared basically with eggs, with consommé, sometimes with milk and cream, or a purée of some kind. *Royales* are simple to make and transform a plain consommé or clear soup.

They are poured into small moulds, cooked in a *bain-marie*, or double boiler, and steamed or baked in a slow oven till firm. When completely cold, they are turned out and cut into shapes of choice. *Royales* are usually served with clear soups, rarely with thick.

The quantities of the recipes following are for 1–1½ litres (2 or 3 pints) of clear soup.

Plain royale

4–6 servings
1·5 dl (¼ pint) milk
2 lightly-beaten eggs
1 teaspoonful flour
salt to taste

Beat the eggs into the milk, add the flour and salt and beat this till smooth. Pour this mixture into a buttered mould and cook in a double boiler until set, about 45 minutes. Allow to get cold, then cut into fancy shapes.

Carrot or Crécy royale

4–6 servings

Cook in butter 1 medium-sized grated carrot, adding a little salt and sugar. Add 1 tablespoonful of béchamel sauce and 2 tablespoonfuls of cream and rub through a sieve. Blend in 4 lightly-beaten egg yolks and proceed as for other *royales.*

Chicken royale

4–6 servings

Pound to a fine pulp 2 tablespoonfuls of cooked white chicken meat. Add 2 tablespoonfuls each of béchamel sauce and cream. Mix into this 4 lightly-beaten egg yolks and continue as for other *royales.*

Fish royale

4–6 servings

Mix 3 tablespoonfuls of cooked and pounded fish with béchamel sauce and 4 lightly-beaten egg yolks. Proceed as for other *royales.* Or use half béchamel and half cream.

Game royale

4–6 servings

Pound to a fine pulp 50 gr (2 oz) of any cooked game; add to this 1½ teaspoonfuls of demi-glaze and 3 tablespoonfuls of clear meat or game stock. Add 2 egg yolks and 1 whole egg, lightly beaten, and continue as for other *royales.*

Girodine royale

4–6 servings

As for plain or carrot *royale,* but with some finely-chopped cooked ham and finely-shredded cooked carrot.

Royale of pea purée

4–6 servings

Blend 2 tablespoonfuls of sifted pea purée with 4 tablespoonfuls of clear meat stock; add salt and sugar. Beat in 1 whole egg and 2 yolks, all lightly beaten, pour into a mould and proceed as for other *royales.*

Tomato royale

4–6 servings

As for plain or carrot *royale,* but substitute tomato juice for milk or consommé. A very few drops of carmine may be added.

Truffle royale

4–6 servings

Finely-chopped truffle with 1½ tablespoonfuls of cold demi-glaze sauce, much reduced and beaten into 3 lightly-beaten egg yolks.

Herbs

The use of herbs in soup really requires some detailed treatment, so I am devoting the next few pages to laying down some general guidelines to this interesting subject.

As we all know, tastes differ. It is obvious, therefore, that the use of spices and herbs must be an individual affair. However, I can offer suggestions to act as a guide. The more one becomes used or addicted to both spices and herbs, the more one may experiment. But there are some rules:

1 Herbs and spices must be fresh. This means buying in small quantities whether you are buying tinned, bottled or fresh spices, or herbs. They should never be kept too long.

2 Use all herbs and spices with care: both are there to stimulate or subtly to enhance the flavour of any dish; they should never be allowed to drown a flavour.

3 When using dried herbs remember to use less. As a rough guide, half a teaspoonful of dried herb and a quarter of a teaspoonful of powdered herb equals two teaspoonfuls of finely-chopped fresh herbs.

4 Crushing or mincing fresh herbs brings out their full

flavour. Roasting such spices as cardamom, or even fine seeds such as cumin, has the same effect.

5 Herbs and spices can be added either at the beginning of cooking time or at the end. Cooks differ on this. Usually I add them at the beginning but there are exceptions to every rule. Do as you please on this point.

Now for a list of those herbs and spices particularly useful for flavouring soups. It looks fairly formidable. Many are regularly used in English cooking; some are new to us; many were once well known but for some reason have lost their popularity. However, like Victorian bric-à-brac, forgotten herbs and spices are creeping back into their own.

Anise

The tiny seeds of the anise herb which, although more or less indigenous to the East and its warm climate, takes kindly (when grown) to our more temperate climes. There are several varieties of this seed, but usually it is a small, greenish-grey seed appearing almost brown. It has a rather sweet, pleasant, aromatic flavour and is used a great deal in confectionery. It also adds much to soups, giving them an entirely new and delightful character. Try anise with mussel, shrimp and other shellfish soups, or with cheese and vegetable soups. Generally a quarter of a teaspoonful is enough flavouring for soup for six people.

Sweet basil

A very versatile herb of which there are some fifty varieties all differing in height, flavour and colour. This, obviously, makes it impossible absolutely to describe it. I grow the Italian and the Indian varieties in my garden (in pots) and they do not look even related. The Indians, by the way, number their variety of basil, locally called *tulsi*, among their sacred plants and attribute to it many healing properties. It is used a great deal in Latin cooking and is excellent in tomato and pea soups and that triumph of cooking, turtle soup. Basically its flavour is between that of the clove and the liquorice – more than that I am not prepared to say – and a leaf or two usually is enough for average flavouring.

Bay leaf

The uses of this well-known herb are manifold. It is the leaf of a large evergreen plant which grows extensively in Mediterranean countries, also very much in Britain and Central America. The odour of the bay leaf is familiar to most of us; it is strong, pungent and rather bitter. One leaf usually is enough for flavouring. But this one leaf, whether fresh or dried, will give an excellent flavour to mutton broth, to all meat soups in fact; to tomato and rice soups, and with vegetable soups, especially beetroot, onion and potato soups.

Caraway

Most of us connect caraway seeds with seedy cake; anyway those old enough to remember this once favourite English cake. Actually it is a herb, a hardy perennial which grows in Asia Minor and is cultivated in many of the European countries, as well as Russia, Syria and some parts of the United States. It is a plant which grows to a height of about two feet, with leaves which resemble those of the carrot – a kind of 'Queen Anne's Lace' in appearance. The fresh leaves, the seeds and the root of this herb all have their own flavours, with the root differing entirely in flavour from the seeds. The roots are very sweet and delicate in flavour, while the leaves have something of the flavour of the seeds, but are far more delicate. The roots may be eaten and boiled as a vegetable, rather like the parsnip, the flavour of which they slightly resemble, and they are served in the same manner, generously buttered. When using caraway leaves in soups, try cabbage and cauliflower soups as well as potato. It can be added to the cooking or used as a lightly sprinkled green garnish.

Caraway seeds

Most of us are on firmer ground with this small, crescent-shaped, highly aromatic and popular little seed. Although we in Britain and America use it mainly in cakes and breads, in many of the European countries we find it in soups and stews. I use it with cabbage, beetroot, turnip and other vegetable soups. It is essential with goulash dishes. Usually a quarter of a teaspoonful of this seed is sufficient for flavouring soup for six – but more can be used.

Cardamom

In the Orient these somewhat irregular angular seeds are called 'the seeds of Paradise'. A member of the ginger family, it grows prolifically along the Indian Malabar coast. The texture of the cardamom is hard and it varies in shape, size and colour. It is usually pungent and aromatic, with perhaps a slight flavour of anise and it is supposed to be stimulating and antiseptic. Cardamom seeds are used in a large number of ways in the East – the Kashmiris use them in very very sweet, milky tea – but they are important in curry dishes and flavour such soups as pea or lentil and, of course, any soup with a curry flavour.

Celery seed

These are the dried fruits of the celery plant and they can be used in many ways in which celery is used as a flavouring. The seeds have the sweetish aromatic flavour of fresh celery and can be added to almost all soups or stock where fresh celery would be used. It is the ground celery seeds which make celery salt.

Chervil

A delicate cooking herb, a member of the parsley family, with a subtle, indescribable flavour with maybe something of tarragon about it. It is one of the ingredients of the French *fines herbes* and it is much used in flavouring continental soups. I would especially recommend it with lettuce, sorrel, watercress, spinach or other green vegetable soups.

Chives

This herb is growing in popularity. Not only does it give subtle flavouring to many of our everyday dishes but it looks so pretty in the garden, with its small rounded, clove-like purplish flower. It can be used either in a soup to give it flavour, or as a garnish. I usually put a few stalks of chives into stocks and use it always with potato soups. It should always be used where only a mild onion flavour is desired; for example, in an asparagus soup or any of the more elegant creamed ones.

Coriander

Both the leaves and the seeds of this lacy-looking herb are used. It is native to Europe and Asia and is called the parsley of the East. It has established itself in some parts of England as a wild plant and grows to a limited degree in Kentucky in the United States. It can be used in soups of many kinds, in beef and mutton broths, but in moderation as its flavour is somewhat stronger than that of parsley. The seeds are extremely aromatic and should be used sparingly.

Cumin seed

An aromatic seed with a slightly bitter flavour. It grows extensively in Mediterranean countries, looks somewhat like the caraway seed, and even the flavour bears a slight resemblance. Cumin does have a stronger flavour and should be used with care, but it can find its place in fish soups and chowders as well as any curry-flavoured or vegetable soups.

Dill

Another member of the vast parsley family. To Americans, I know, dill means pickles; the British use it a little, but the Russians would find life impossible without dill. I use it a great deal in my fish soups. Its flavour is somewhat sharp, warm and aromatic and, curiously enough, it is particularly good with mutton broth. Otherwise it adds a lot to such soups as bean, beetroot, tomato, vegetable, turnip and cabbage. There are, by the way, both the ground and the whole seeds and these are interchangeable.

Fennel

This was once a favourite English garden herb and used in fish dishes. There is the wild and the cultivated variety, but both varieties have the same mild liquorice flavour. It is a very pleasant and pretty herb. The large so-called Florentine fennel (*finocchio*) is used as a vegetable, which indeed it is.

Fennel seeds

These are the dried, almost ripe fruit of the herb, another seed resembling the caraway. (It is as well to have one's herb bottles very clearly labelled as so many of these seeds look alike.) It can be used as a flavouring where the fresh fennel would be used and its flavour is becoming increasingly popular. It can be used as it is or its flavour enhanced by roasting. The flavour of all fennel is mildly liquorice. Incidentally, it used to be called in America 'Meetin' Seed' because the Puritans used to nibble it in church.

Garlic

For years this herb has been out of favour – it became synonymous with a bad smell. But it is now enjoying a tremendous come-back, everyone trying to prove whether used in moderation or to excess it has no after effects. An ancient member of the lily or onion family, garlic has a long and honourable history. It is dead-white in colour and is divided into segments called cloves. It can be used in so many soups it is not necessary to name any one in particular.

Ginger

This is the root of a sweet-smelling and handsome plant which grows wild and looks something like a wild iris or canna. It is a deep creamy colour and grows in tropical areas. Some of the finest ginger comes from Jamaica and China. The part we eat is the washed and dried root. It is irregular in shape and looks something like the Jerusalem artichoke. Its flavour and aroma is deliciously pungent. It is a pity that it is so much used in its ground or powdered form, for those of us who know it in its fresh, juicy 'green' state realize that its flavour bears little resemblance to ground ginger. When the fresh ginger is not available, I suggest using the dried ginger and soaking it until it becomes soft.

Leek

Another member of the important lily or onion family. Used fresh it has a mild but delicious flavour. The herb develops long stalks underground and broad flat leaves above. Although its flavour is mild, its aroma is strong. On the whole cooks do not use the green stalk as much as they could. Perhaps because where I live leeks are extremely expensive, we tend not to waste an inch of them. I use leek in all stocks and it is especially good mixed into vegetable soups. It is, of course, the mainstay of Vichyssoise.

Marigold

This is unquestionably more popular as a garden flower than as a herb. Both in its dried form or fresh, it can be used to advantage in broths and soups – its effect in soups is astonishing. In Jersey it is an ingredient in their favourite eel soup and it is particularly good in chicken broth.

Marjoram

Another herb native to the Mediterranean countries, often used as a substitute for sage since it is less pungent. It is greatly used in Latin dishes, especially Portuguese and

Italian, and is recommended in such soups as tomato, potato, onion and turtle. The cultivated marjoram is much sweeter than its wild counterpart. It can be bought fresh and dried and, when growing in the garden, it gives a wonderful fragrance. It is a small, rather bushy plant with greyish-green leaves.

Mint

This is probably the most widely used herb in the world. There are several kinds of this very aromatic plant which can be used in a large number of ways, in pea soups, for instance, and as a garnish in tomato and carrot soups.

Oregano

Not much used in Britain but a popular Italian herb used a lot in America. It is a lovely plant which grows into a high leafy bush. There are several varieties of this herb all of which are sweet and pungent in flavour. Use in bean and tomato soups.

Paprika

It is often imagined that paprika pepper is hot. True paprika pepper is a reddish-deep orange colour with a sweet, rich flavour. It must be carefully prepared and the best comes from Hungary and Spain. It can be used in numerous soups, i.e. vegetable, chicken and any type of goulash soup.

Parsley

Few people evidently realize that there are over thirty varieties of this popular herb. Its flavour is so well known that it is taken for granted. It can be used in flavouring almost all kinds of soups and is particularly good as a garnish for fish, potato and tomato soups.

Rosemary

For remembrance. A sweet-scented shrubby plant which can be used both fresh and dried. It is one of the most loved of all herbs. The dried herb is almost as good as the fresh and it has many uses. As far as soups are concerned, it is used to advantage in chicken, pea and spinach soups. Cauliflower soup is greatly enhanced garnished with a sprinkling of either fresh or dried rosemary.

Saffron

An expensive spice produced from the dried stigma of the saffron crocus. It is indigenous to Asia and cultivated for the nutty flavour of the seed. It takes something in the region of 75,000 hand-picked blossoms to make one pound of true saffron – and there are a number of forgeries on the market. However, a little saffron goes a long way and can be used in fish soups, of the bouillabaisse type, as well as rice soups.

Sage

There are several hundred different kinds of sage which can be used either fresh or dried. It marries agreeably with fish and creamed soups.

Sesame seed

The product of a small, annual plant which grows extensively in the East. There are several varieties. Its flavour is intriguing, vaguely reminding one of toasted almonds. Excellent in creamed soups and sprinkled on buttered toast or rolls used as a garnish to soup.

Tarragon

Another well-known herb with an intriguing flavour, very pungent. It was one of the 'little dragon-herbs' which had a reputation for curing victims of wounds caused by these ferocious creatures. It can be used in a number of soups but is especially good in a mushroom and chicken soup, consommé, tomato and turtle soups. If using fresh tarragon leaves, most soups can take several whole leaves.

Thyme

Although the British claim this herb as their own – 'I know a bank whereon the wild thyme blows' as sung by their national bard – it was actually brought to Britain by the Romans. There are several varieties. It is grown extensively in Italy, Greece and Switzerland and can be used in fish and meat soups, in moderation, vegetable (and in particular beetroot) soups.

Turmeric

A fleshy root stalk containing a bright yellow dye, it is a principal ingredient of many Oriental dishes. Its flavour is faintly resinous and it can be used to advantage in a soup which lacks flavour. But remember that it is a dye and also gives soup a strong curry flavour as this ingredient is one of those most used in curry powder.

Watercress

This peppery little perennial is a delight as a garnish for a number of soups. It can also be made into a soup of its own. It marries well with chowders, fish, creamed soups as well as the herb soups. It is invaluable as a garnish.

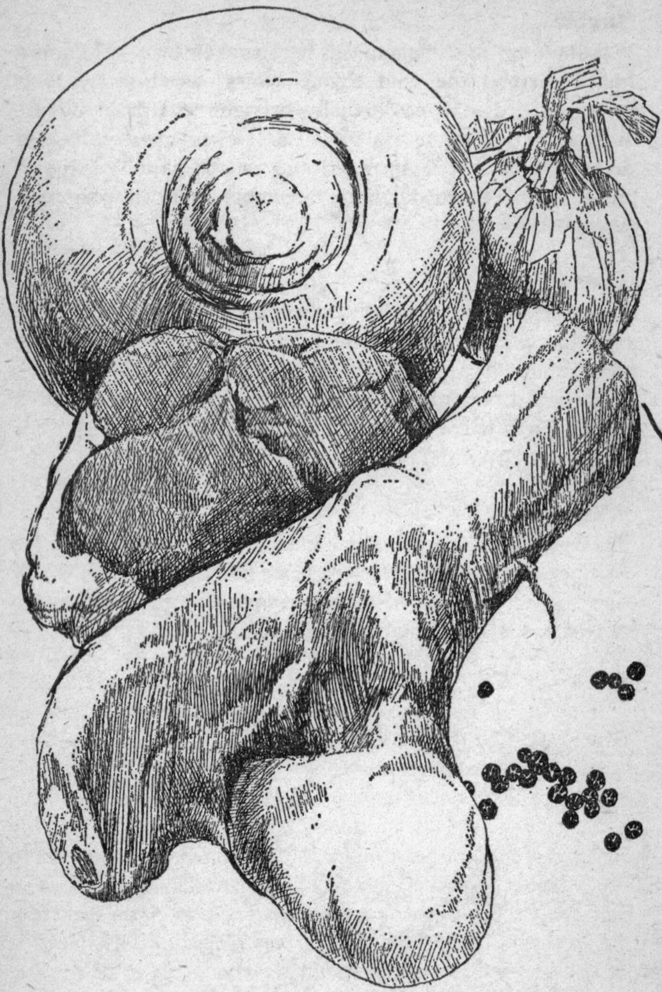

Stocks and clear soups

The chief art of soup making is to produce a good basic stock and to utilize scraps wisely. Stock is the foundation of almost all good soups (and many sauces) and is the liquid obtained by simmering down various nutritious substances. Simmering is of vital importance. Good stocks cannot be made quickly, although it is not necessary to take more than four to five hours over their preparation. Alexandre Dumas called this simmering 'to make the pot smile' (*faire sourire le pot-au-feu*) and declared that this expression was a common French one which had not found its way into the dictionary; promising, however, that if ever he were included among the forty Immortals of the French Academy he would have it included in the *Dictionnaire de l'Académie*. Unhappily he never was, so the expression never became official.

There was a time not so long ago when a stockpot was always simmering on the kitchen stove. Often these stockpots became culinary dustbins, merrily collecting bacteria, which should never happen. As a result, stomachs suffered and the stockpot finally fell into disrepute.

Nowadays there are still many of us who make our own stocks, and one hopes that we are greater in number than the sale of commercially produced packets would suggest. We know now that four or five hours of slow cooking will give us a good extract, that this extract or stock should be poured into a non-metal container as soon as it is ready and cooled before being put into a refrigerator. It was the length of time that stocks were left in saucepans which turned them into breeding grounds for bacteria.

How much stock you can make and how long it can be kept

depends primarily on the size of the household refrigerator. I have a very large refrigerator, plus a small freezer. As far as I am concerned, these two items of kitchen equipment are as important as the kitchen stove.

I think even in these somewhat hectic modern days of instant cooking and eating that the value of the stockpot as a basis of soup and good eating cannot be overlooked. No one pretends that to make soup from scratch is as simple as opening a tin or pouring water over a powder, but the results are entirely different. I have no axe to grind, nor am I 'anti' tinned or packaged soups, but I know that they are not as good as my stock-flavoured soups. However, I need not dwell on this point. I must assume that the readers of this book make stocks because they want to make good soups.

The best materials will always give the finest results. This rule applies to most things we do. Many gourmets still argue that no ingredient is too fine for the stockpot. Another point, this time without argument, is that the preparation of stock begins with *cold* water; that this, plus meat and bones, is brought to a slow boil, taking about one hour, and the stock then simmered for four or five hours.

Good stock cannot be cooked quickly. This is something which cannot be emphasized enough. Time is essential, for much is lost if boiling is allowed. This solidifies the albumen and causes scum. Some scum will form on the liquid in any case and it is usual to clear this off. There are many cooks who argue that it is better to let this scum remain, for in it remains some of the stock. However, a truly clear stock must be skimmed.

A stock can be made and used the same day; but basic stocks are much better made at least one day before they are required. After the stock is cooked, strain it into a china or porcelain bowl, and, as soon as it is cool, put it into a refrigerator or a very, very cold place (a cool larder is not cold enough). This preserves the stock, keeps it fresh and also causes the fat to rise to the top and form a thick layer. This layer must be removed before the soup is heated again. Every particle of fat must be removed so that the stock is very clear.

The old custom of making a stock and simmering it merrily for days – in some people's minds a stockpot is never empty from year to year – is to be discounted. Not only is this unhealthy, but no good cook would be foolish enough to reboil food that has lost its goodness. I remember in Jamaica, after an all-night country dance in one of the so-called Great Houses, we were given pepperpot soup. 'This,' said my hostess cheerfully and to impress, 'has been cooking for a hundred years. An old Jamaican custom,' she added. In that heat! The thought was appalling. Fortunately I do not believe all I hear, and ate happily; but there is no doubt that they used, at one time, to cook this pepperpot soup (it is more of a stew) for a very long time: and this may have accounted for a lot of Jamaican stomach disorders.

Stocks are flavoured or unflavoured, the latter being minus vegetables. Unflavoured stock was once highly rated for its keeping qualities, also as being excellent for invalids. Even when flavouring a stock, it should never be overdone, for this would ruin the final flavouring which is to be the soup.

There are some old-fashioned rules in stock making which still hold good. The quality of the bones and meat should be good and fresh. Most butchers will still let you have bones, and most genuine butchers will saw up the bones. Breaking and chopping the bones causes the gelatine to be released quickly, and an abundance of this means that the stock jellifies easily. Two ounces of fresh bones contain as much gelatine as a pound of meat. For a perfectly clear stock it is generally considered better to use one part veal and one part beef. The flesh of the mature animal is more nutritious than that of the young one. My butcher often lets me have bits of meat cheaply and the odd sheep's head or tongue. Anyway, fresh uncooked meat undoubtedly makes the best stock, the glutinous matter adding strength, richness and thickness to the soup which will be the end product.

Much of the meat, chicken or game used in making a stock can be used as a main dish (like the French *pot-au-feu* or Scotch broth). Certainly old fowl makes not only a good stock but can also, with a little doctoring, be used as a main dish. If this is done, tie up the bird (or meat) neatly for easier cutting or serving. I usually wrap muslin round a chicken or duck which is to be used for a dual purpose. Even vegetables which flavour a stock can be utilized, served as they are, or puréed.

Consommé is made by simmering raw meat and bones in the already cleared stock until all the goodness is extracted, and its flavour is decided mainly by the vegetables cooked with it. Many a clear stock masquerades as a consommé. Clear stock, however clear, is not consommé; but if care is taken in removing all scum and fat from the stock, the result is as clear and of as good a colour as most of us would want. For many soups, the two are interchangeable and much of the pleasure of both clear soup and consommé is that they should be limpid.

Brown stock

1·5 kg (3 lb) shin of beef, with bones
a few giblets (optional)
1 hambone (optional)
450 gr (1 lb) knuckle of veal
4·8 litres (8 pints) cold water
bouquet garni
12 peppercorns
2 chopped carrots
2 leeks
2 chopped celery stalks
2 chopped onions
1 chopped turnip
1 tablespoonful salt

Cut the meat into large pieces, chop the bones, ham and beef (if the butcher has not done this for you) and clean the giblets. Spread the bones and meat in a large roasting pan, add the onions, carrots and turnip and let them all brown in a hot oven. This will take about 30–40 minutes. Put the browned ingredients into a large saucepan, add the remaining ingredients (except salt and peppercorns), bring gently to the boil and cook slowly – not less than 3 or 4 hours. Add the peppercorns and salt after 2 hours of cooking. Skim the stock frequently. When ready, strain through a sieve and leave overnight. In the morning skim off the layer of fat which will have formed on the top. When taking the stock from the bowl to use, be careful not to include the sediment which usually settles at the bottom.

If a less brown stock is required, omit the pre-roasting of the meat, etc. The strength of the stock will be the same, the colour paler. Meat and bones can be used for a second but weaker stock.

Brown bone stock

1·5–2 kg (3–4 lb) beef bones
900 gr (2 lb) veal bones
1 large chopped carrot
1 chopped turnip or parsnip
3 chopped celery stalks
parsley to taste
1 tablespoonful salt
12 peppercorns
4·8 litres (8 pints) water

Saw the bones into small pieces. Spread these out in a large roasting pan, covered with the carrot, onion and turnip or parsnip. Roast in a hot oven for 30–40 minutes. When browned, put everything into a large saucepan with water, celery and parsley. Bring gently to the boil, simmer for 2 hours, add salt and peppercorns, and continue cooking as long as possible.

If a roasted chicken carcass is available, add this. Strain the soup, leave overnight and, next morning, skim off the layer of fat. When using, avoid the sediment at the bottom of the bowl.

Bones can be used for a second stock.

Consommé

225 gr (½ lb) shin of beef
½ bay leaf
1 peeled, chopped onion
1 peeled, chopped carrot
1 sprig thyme
2·5–3·5 litres (4–6 pints) cold stock
1 sprig marjoram
2 egg whites and 2 eggshells
1 stick celery
1 glass sherry
12 peppercorns
salt, sugar

Remove all the fat from the stock. Mince the meat finely. Whip the egg whites and crush the shells. Put these ingredients, with the stock, vegetables and the herbs, into a saucepan. Whisk it over the fire until it begins to boil. Let it simmer for 10 minutes, then add the sherry. Bring it again to the boil, take it from the heat and let it stand for 5 minutes. Strain slowly through a cloth. Return to the pan, reheat, add salt to taste, then the peppercorns and a small lump of sugar. It is now ready to serve, a perfectly clear and beautifully-flavoured consommé which may be garnished to taste. It all takes about 45 minutes. When the stock is cold, skim off the fat and correct the seasoning. For each 1·2 litres (2 pints) of stock use 1 egg white and 1 eggshell. Break up the egg white and the shell together, add this to the cold stock and bring it slowly to the boil, stirring all the while. Let it boil for 3 or 4 minutes, still stirring; lower the heat so that the stock barely simmers for 20 minutes. Skim off all particles that have risen to the top, strain the stock through two thicknesses of cheese cloth. The stock should be perfectly clear and may be served hot or cold.

Consommé

A clear beef stock garnished with strips of cooked cucumber, diced tomato *royale* (*see* page 40) and/or sliced fried tomatoes.

Consommé Bavière

Light consommé garnished with cheese-flavoured semolina dumplings (*see* page 32).

Consommé brunoise
An everyday consommé garnished with diced, cooked carrots, turnips, leeks, etc.

Consommé chasseur
A rather dark consommé sometimes made of game stock, garnished with game *quenelles* (*see* page 37).

Consommé Condorcet
A clear game stock with game *quenelles*, asparagus tips, diced foie gras and truffles.

Consommé Demidoff
This is a clear consommé, garnished with diced carrot, turnip, cooked green peas, diced truffles and minute chicken *quenelles* or dumplings.

Consommé d'Esclignac
A light consommé with minute cooked turnip balls and diced plain *royale*. Sometimes made of chicken stock with tiny *quenelles* and the turnips.

Consommé diplomate
A consommé garnished with chicken dumplings (*see* pages 31–2) shaped like tiny sausages. When the soup is boiling, crushed tapioca is added, to taste. The dumplings are cooked in the soup and take only a few minutes.

Consommé d'Orléans
A rather dark consommé with small green and white *quenelles* – the green ones are spinach-coloured.

Consommé Dubarry
A consommé garnished with diced custard *royale* flavoured with finely-chopped sweet almonds, very small pieces of cooked cauliflower, and boiled rice.

Consommé duchesse

A consommé sprinkled with sago when hot, cooked until this is transparent and garnished with strips of chicken breast.

Consommé Duclair

A consommé garnished with stuffed pancakes. Mince some tender cooked chicken meat, pound this with 3 filleted anchovies, add salt and pepper to taste, and moisten with a béchamel sauce. Make some very thin pancakes, to any favourite recipe, spread half of these with the mixture, cover with the remaining pancakes, making sandwiches. Cut these into shapes and drop them into soup cups or in a soup tureen and add boiling soup.

Consommé Dustan

A rather dark, clear stock garnished with cooked white haricot beans.

Consommé grande duchesse

A white stock with cheese and anchovy *quenelles* and shredded cooked chicken and tongue.

Consommé impératrice

A very clear, very strong consommé to which at the last moment poached and neatly-trimmed eggs are added. (A great pick-me-up, said to have been first made for the Empress Eugénie when tired after a hunt at Fontainebleau.)

Consommé Madère

8 servings

A recipe from a century-old, dog-eared cookery book found, curiously enough, in India, where strong drink and wines once flowed, and livers and choleric colonels abounded.

2·5 litres (4 pints) chicken consommé
1 bottle Madeira
thin slices of lime or lemon

Pour the consommé and the wine into a large saucepan, bring to the boil, pour into a tureen and serve garnished with lime slices.

In India it is the lime which is used, hardly ever the lemon, although lemons grow easily. Most Indian cooks I have met are convinced that lemons have no culinary value at all – quite the reverse of the Sicilians' conviction.

The quantity of wine used in this soup appears excessive to me. I prefer a proportion of one good wineglass of wine to every 1·2 litres (2 pints), otherwise the flavour of the wine overpowers the stock. I suspect that the admonition of an old cook 'that too much wine in the soup will certainly make you intoxicated if not sick' might well apply. Perhaps our Anglo-Indian forefathers could take it.

Consommé Madrilène

6 servings

900 gr (2 lb) ripe tomatoes
1 chopped onion
1–2 stalks chopped celery
1 chopped turnip
bouquet garni
6 peppercorns
salt if required
1·8 litres (3 pints) stock, first or second
225 gr (½ lb) lean minced meat
2 egg whites, lightly beaten, and 2 crushed shells
1 sugar lump

Cut the tomatoes into quarters, put with the remaining vegetables into a saucepan, add the stock, bouquet garni and peppercorns, and cook until the tomatoes are soft. Mix the meat with enough water to form a lump. Put this into the pan. Add the egg whites and shells. Whisk the soup until it comes to the boil, lower the heat and simmer for 30 minutes. Strain through a fine sieve or cloth, return it to the pan and reheat. Add salt, if required, and sugar. Garnish with croûtons or peeled, diced tomatoes and chopped chives. About half a cupful of Madeira may also be added. This consommé will, if iced, turn to jelly. It should then be broken up, served in bouillon cups and generously sprinkled with finely-chopped green herbs.

Consommé Metternich

A game consommé, garnished with sliced artichoke hearts, strips of cooked game fillet and sherry to taste. Tinned or bottled artichokes can be used.

Consommé mille-fanti

8 servings

25 gr (1 oz) soft breadcrumbs
25 gr (1 oz) grated Parmesan cheese
salt and cayenne pepper
2 well-beaten eggs
2·5 litres (4 pints) consommé

Mix the breadcrumbs and cheese and add the eggs, salt and pepper. Bring the consommé to the boil. Drop the mixture into this through a funnel, like egg rain (*see* page 33). Stir with a whisk while doing so. It requires some dexterity and an extra pair of hands is useful. Cover the pan and simmer for 6 minutes. When ready to serve, stir the soup with a whisk.

Consommé Monte-Carlo

A consommé into which are dropped tiny chicken dumplings (*see* pages 31–2) and fresh, finely-chopped chervil and lettuce.

Consommé Nesselrode

8 servings

1 whole egg and 2 yolks, well beaten
1·5 dl (¼ pint) cream
3 tablespoonfuls chestnut purée
pinch of sugar, salt and pepper

Mix all these ingredients to make a chestnut *royale.* Pour the mixture into a buttered, shallow dish, put this into a pan of warm water and bake in a slow oven until the custard sets firmly. Let this cool, then cut into diamonds or other fancy shapes. Drop these into a game consommé (or other type), add white wine to taste and finely-shredded orange peel. This soup is often garnished with strips of fillet of cooked breast of game.

Consommé nouvelle reine

This one is fun. Have ready 2·5 litres (4 pints) of chicken consommé. Prepare 1·5 dl (¼ pint) aspic jelly; just as it is beginning to set, break into it two or three leaves of gold leaf. (This is available at Indian or Pakistani stores.) Let this set, then cut into small cubes. Make some chicken dumpling mixture (*see* pages 31–2), shape into balls, putting a cube of aspic in the middle of each dumpling. Close it up. Each dumpling should be large enough for the diner to cut it with his spoon, thus letting the gold come sparkling out.

Consommé poissonnière

A well-flavoured clear fish stock with fish *quenelles.*

Consommé Portugaise

5 servings
1·2 litres (2 pints) consommé
12 French plums
salt, cayenne pepper
1 thinly-cut leek (white part only)

Wash the plums and put them into a saucepan with cold water to cover. Add salt and pepper to taste, let them come to the boil, and drain. Heat half the consommé, add plums, cover and simmer the leeks in this for a few minutes. Add the remaining stock, bring to the boil and skim off the fat. Put the plums either into a tureen or into bowls, heat all the stock together and pour this over the plums. Serve hot, with croûtons offered separately.

Consommé princesse

A rather modest princess, it would appear! A consommé into which, just before serving, are dropped leaves of chervil, match-like strips of potatoes and little chicken *quenelles* (*see* pages 31–2).

Consommé Renaissance (Spinach *Royale*)

1 serving

1·5 dl (¼ pint) cooked, sieved spinach
14 gr (½ oz) butter
1 tablespoonful cream
2 eggs
salt, pepper

Heat the butter in a saucepan, add the spinach, blend, then add the cream and the eggs. Add salt and pepper to taste. Pour into a buttered mould and steam till firm. Leave till cold and cut into dice. Serve this as a garnish to consommé plus some cooked peas, diced turnip and carrot.

Consommé Trianon

A consommé served with diced tomato, spinach and plain *royale*.

Consommé veneur

A consommé with a custard *royale*, coloured with a few drops of cochineal and cut into diamonds. Add finely-shredded truffle, lettuce and fresh tarragon.

Consommé vermicelli

A consommé into which boiled vermicelli is dropped and served very hot. About 25 gr (1 oz) vermicelli to each 1·8 litres (2 pints) of stock.

Consommé vert pré

A consommé to which is added just enough spinach juice to give it colour and, immediately before serving, finely-chopped green fresh herbs. Can be served hot or cold.

Celery consommé

4 servings

1·2 litres (2 pints) clarified stock or consommé
1 head celery
salt, pepper
croûtons

Clean the celery, chop it coarsely and use all of it, including the leaves. Put this into a saucepan, add the consommé and bring to the boil. Lower the heat and simmer for about 30 minutes, till the celery is tender and its flavour has fully penetrated the stock. Add salt and pepper, if required, strain and serve hot, garnished with croûtons.

Herb consommé

6 servings

1·8 litres (3 pints) clarified chicken stock
2 tablespoonfuls finely-chopped chives
1 dessertspoonful chopped fresh tarragon
salt, pepper
slices of lemon

Bring the stock to the boil and add the herbs. Take the soup from the fire, leave for a couple of minutes, strain and return it to the pan. Add salt and pepper, if needed. Reheat and serve the soup hot, garnished with thin slices of lemon. Although this soup is obviously at its best with a stock, if only the herbs and bouillon cubes or tinned consommé are available, the herbs will do a lot for both.

Tomato and orange consommé (USA)

Combine equal quantities of strained, fresh orange juice and tomato consommé. Add lemon juice to flavour, salt, pepper and a dash of celery salt. Bring this to the boil. The soup may be served either hot or very cold and garnished with finely-chopped mint or chives.

Chicken soup with eggs (*Zuppa Pavese*) (Italy)

1 serving

1 slice fried bread per person
grated Parmesan cheese
1 egg per person
salt, pepper
boiling, clear chicken broth

Into each soup plate or cup put a slice of freshly-fried bread. Sprinkle this generously with cheese. Carefully drop in 1 whole shelled egg, salt and pepper to taste. Cover this with absolutely boiling stock – it must be boiling, otherwise the egg does not cook properly. Many people prefer to poach the eggs first, but this completely changes the character of the soup; still good, but for my taste less interesting. This soup appears on the menu of every Italian restaurant.

Mock turtle soup

Many of the recipes for mock turtle soup are long and arduous; some use a pig's head as well as a calf's head. This is sometimes objected to because it leaves the soup greasy and a great deal of skimming is required. My recipe, from my grandmother's note book, produces a good and not at all greasy soup.

Take half a calf's head, 100 gr (¼ lb) butter, very lean ham, 2 tablespoonfuls finely-chopped parsley, a little minced thyme, sweet marjoram and basil, 2 chopped onions, some chopped mushrooms, 2 chopped shallots, 50 gr (2 oz) flour, 16 forcemeat balls (each about the size of a nutmeg), salt and pepper to suit the taste, the juice of 1 lemon, 1 Seville orange, 1 dessertspoonful pounded sugar, and 3·5 litres (6 pints) of the best bone stock.

All of this is cooked happily together until the meat is tender. I omit the forcemeat balls as I think it is rich enough without them – the soup is strained and, if required, forcemeat balls can be served with it – otherwise flavour it simply with a little Madeira. A second stock may be made from the above ingredients.

Mutton broth

Lean meat is the best for any broth. For this recipe, 1–1·5 kg (2–3 lb) scrag end of neck is suitable. Put this into a saucepan and add cold water (just over 6 dl (1 pint) for each 450 gr (1 lb) of meat if a good, strong broth is required, or double the amount for a weak broth). Put this on to a slow fire to heat gradually, simmer gently and remove scum. When all the scum has been removed and the meat is tender, it should be taken from the pan, put aside but kept hot. At this point, barley, oatmeal or rice, a carrot, turnip, onion or leek can be added (all the vegetables being cleaned, peeled, etc., and cut into small neat pieces). Salt and pepper are added to taste. Let this continue cooking for roughly another hour. In the meantime, reheat the meat and serve this separately as a main dish. Serve the soup with the vegetables.

Orange bortsch (USA)

8–10 servings

675 gr (1½ lb) beetroot
1·2 litres (2 pints) strained beef stock
6 dl (1 pint) strained fresh tomato juice
1 teaspoonful salt
½ teaspoonful ground pepper
6 dl (1 pint) strained fresh orange juice

Peel and grate the beetroot coarsely. Put into a pan with the stock, salt and pepper, and bring to the boil; lower the heat and cook gently for about 30 minutes. Strain and put aside the beetroot. Add the tomato juice to the soup; return this to the pan, add salt and pepper, if required, bring to the boil, add the orange juice, stir and bring once more to the boil. This soup may be served hot or iced, and should be garnished with sour cream and finely-chopped chives.

The grated beetroot can be made into a cream of beetroot soup. To do this, add stock, rub the soup through a sieve, or purée in a blender to ensure a smooth texture. Add salt and pepper and return the soup to the fire for reheating. Beat

2 egg yolks, whisk these into about 1·5 dl (¼ pint) cream and serve hot, garnished with finely-chopped chives.

Should any of the orange bortsch be left over, it can be jellied – add gelatine as required, the quantity depending on how much bortsch there is. Sherry may be added to give additional flavour and, if you are feeling generous, have a garnish of either red or black caviar. It does not have to be the best Beluga.

Pot-au-feu

To include or not to include – I gave myself a Hamlet-like complex. Surely, I told myself, everyone who knows anything about anything has a recipe for this splendid soup, and yet, how not to include this dish of national importance in France in a book devoted to soups? *Pot-au-feu* won: that *pot-au-feu* which is on the simmer from early morning to dinnertime, into which many loose, unconsidered trifles find a way.

There are no hard and fast rules for the preparation of a *pot-au-feu.* It is like making apple pie, some like it plain, others primrose-flavoured. It is all a matter of taste. In the making of all national dishes, every cook has his own tricks. I have at least a dozen 'authentic' recipes for a *pot-au-feu*; I do not doubt there are a dozen more. All I shall claim here is that my recipe is typical and obeys the rules.

10–12 servings

1·5–2 kg (3–4 lb) rump, shoulder, or round of beef
3·5 litres (6 pints) water
450 gr (1 lb) beef bones
bouquet garni
3–4 each carrots, turnips and leeks
1 clove garlic
1 parsnip
1 small cabbage
4 onions, each stuck with a clove
12 peppercorns
salt

Wash the meat in cold water, put it into a pot, add water, bones, and bouquet garni. Bring this to a quick boil, skim till all the fat has disappeared and the stock is clear. Lower the heat and continue cooking for an hour. Prepare the vegetables according to type – peel, scrape, etc. Slice the leek lengthwise and tie the pieces together – it is easier to take them out later. Cut the remaining vegetables into large pieces of more or less equal size. (If the vegetables are small, leave them whole.) Add the vegetables to the meat. Add salt, garlic and peppercorns and simmer the lot for at least 4 hours. Take out the meat, strain the broth into a soup tureen, chop the vegetables (but not the cabbage) into sizeable pieces for the soup and add these. Serve the soup. Slice the meat as required and serve it with the cabbage.

Celery and other vegetables may also be added. The soup may also be liberally sprinkled with chopped parsley, or the meat may be served surrounded by all the vegetables and the soup perfectly clear. Yet again, the meat can be served with French bread and green salad, and the soup with all of the vegetables, including the cabbage, as a substantial first course.

Turtle soup

The papers had a bill of fare commencing with 'four hundred tureens of turtle soup, each containing five pints', and concluding with the pineapples and ices of the dessert. (W. M. Thackeray)

The turtle or sea-tortoise is to be found in warm waters. The green turtles are those sought to make soup for the Lord Mayor's Banquet and other such feasts. Even in Victorian days it was considered expensive and too difficult for making in private homes. If turtle soup was wanted at home, it could be bought, around 70 years or so ago, for about a guinea a quart.

The turtles from which true turtle soup is made (if it still is) were sent alive from the West Indies, and they would vary in weight from 15–250 kg (30 to 500 lb) each. At an average cost of two shillings a pound at the turn of the century, the turtles obviously were a profitable cargo.

It was in Jamaica, long years ago, that I sampled turtle soup for the first time. There were other delicacies as well, turtle eggs and turtle steaks, the latter somewhat resembling veal or mild beef. The turtle soup the islanders produced was superb, especially when cooked with that Victorian essential to turtle soup cooking, a bottle of Madeira.

1. From fresh turtle meat: USA, where turtles are less rare than in Britain.

4 servings

1·2 litres (2 pints) dark stock
2 slightly-beaten egg whites
½ lemon rind, shredded
450 gr (1 lb) diced turtle meat
salt, pepper
¼ cup Madeira or dry sherry

Cook the meat in enough water to cover till tender. Take it from the pan and dice into very small pieces.

Combine the stock with the liquid formed from cooking the turtle meat. Add the rind and the egg whites and bring this to boiling point, whisking constantly with a wire whisk. Simmer for 5 minutes, then leave 15 minutes to drain. Strain through double cheese cloth. Return to the pan, add the diced meat and reheat without boiling. Add salt and pepper, and the wine immediately before serving.

2. Clear Turtle Soup with dried turtle.

10–12 servings

225 gr (½ lb) sun-dried turtle
5 litres (8 pints) clear stock
2 each small carrots, celery stalks, onions, peeled and chopped
1 each leek and turnip, peeled and chopped
20 peppercorns, 3 cloves, 1 blade mace (tied in a muslin bag
salt, cayenne pepper
bouquet garni
juice of ½ lemon and 1 sprig fresh tarragon
2 glasses sherry and 1 brandy or Madeira

Wash the turtle meat and soak it for three days, changing the water each day. Put the meat with the stock, vegetables, bouquet garni and spice bag into a large saucepan, bring this to the boil and skim thoroughly. Lower the heat and simmer the soup for 8 hours or longer. Add more stock, if necessary. Strain and remove as much fat as possible. Put the meat aside to cool. When cool enough to handle, cut into square pieces. (At this point, for a very clear soup, it should be clarified in the usual manner with minced beef and egg whites; otherwise it can be left as it is.) Bring the soup once more to the boil, add the lemon juice and tarragon and simmer gently for 1 hour. Strain the soup once more through a cloth or very fine sieve; reheat, add the sherry, brandy and the pieces of turtle.

Season with salt and cayenne pepper (if required) and serve.

Rice and lemon soup (Greece)

8 servings

100 gr (4 oz) rice
2·5 litres (4 pints) chicken stock
3 egg yolks
juice of 1 lemon
salt, pepper

Bring the stock to the boil, throw in the rice, add salt and pepper to taste and continue to cook rapidly for 15 minutes. Whisk the egg yolks, add the lemon juice and continue beating till the mixture is smooth, even frothy. Lower the heat of the soup, stir in the egg and lemon sauce; simmer, stirring all the time to avoid curdling, for 2 minutes. Take the pan from the fire, cover it and leave for 5 minutes before serving the soup.

Rice soup (Turkey)

8 servings

100 gr (4 oz) rice
2·5 litres (4 pints) chicken stock
salt, pepper
1·5 dl (¼ pint) cream
butter
finely-chopped parsley

Wash the rice thoroughly, scald it in boiling water for 5 minutes, drain and cook in half the boiling stock for 15 minutes. When very soft, rub it through a sieve. Return this to the pan, add the remaining stock, salt and pepper to taste. Reheat, stir in the cream and about 50 gr (2 oz) butter. Sprinkle with finely-chopped parsley and serve hot.

Venetian soup (Italy)

6 servings

1·8 litres (3 pints) cold, strained clear stock
4–5 tablespoonfuls cream
3 egg yolks
6 slices hot toasted or fried bread

Pour the stock into a saucepan. Beat the egg yolks with the cream, stir this into the stock and gradually bring it almost to the boil. Take at once from the fire. Put a slice of bread into each soup bowl, add the hot soup immediately and serve.

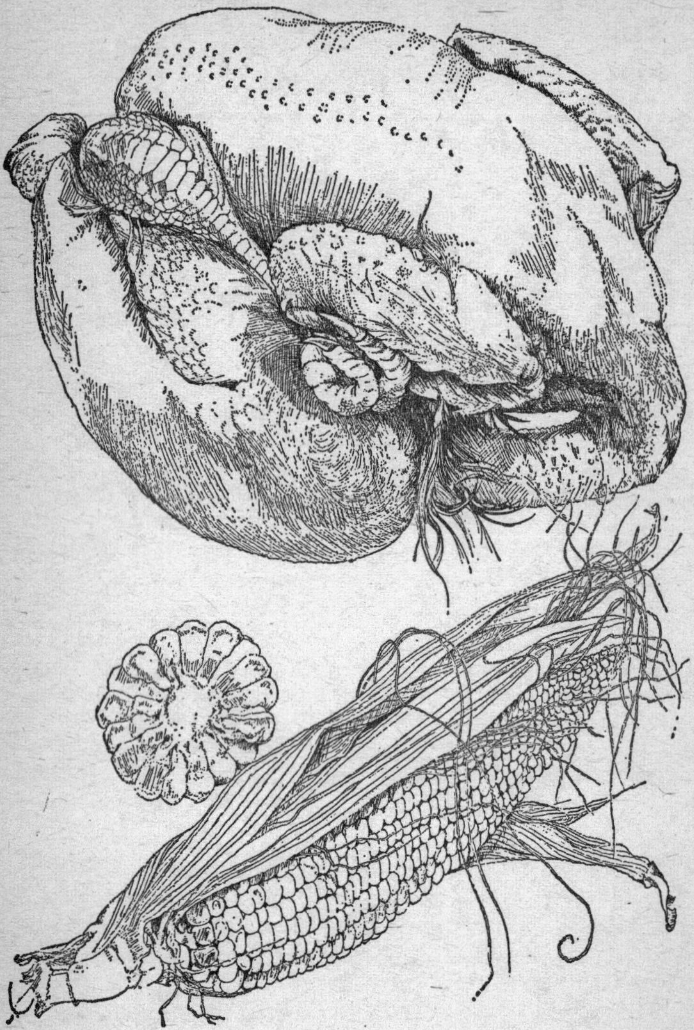

Thick soups and vegetable soups

Thick soups

There are two basic types of thick soup, those thickened with eggs and cream or with a flour and butter roux, and those which are thickened by the process of being rubbed through a sieve or puréed in a blender. The French very properly recognize this difference in thick soups and distinguish between them, the former being *potage lié*, the latter purée.

There is also something known as *potage purée*, which is a homely soup, fairly thin in consistency, garnished with vegetables or whatever is to hand. It is an extremely economical soup for the pennywise housekeeper as well as being delicious. For instance, any remains of meat, poultry, game or fish can be put into a pan, water or second stock added, and the whole simmered in the usual manner of preparing a stock. The bones (if any) are then removed, and the rest is rubbed through a sieve or puréed in the blender. If the consistency is too thick, it is diluted with stock, water or milk and reheated and garnished. Salt and pepper is added to taste and, when available (and it usually is), wine is added as a fillip. If the leftovers are game, it must be red wine, but otherwise sherry or Marsala is best.

Soups thickened with an egg and cream liaison are usually elegant soups which can be served formally. Other types, which have a peasant stamp about them, should be reserved for informal entertaining, to be followed simply by cheese and bread or salads as a main course.

In my opinion, all thick soups are good for the morale, if not, perhaps, for the figure.

There are, further, a number of heavy soups based on vegetable stock and these, for simplicity's sake, have been included in this chapter.

Vegetable soups, which can be equally nourishing, sustaining and attractive, are probably the most simple and surely the cheapest of their kind. As such, they are often misunderstood and certainly underrated. Many people feel that, given a pot of water, some seasonings, herbs and a handful of vegetables, they have a vegetable soup. This is not the complete picture.

As with all dishes, the better the ingredients the finer the results. This reasoning has made French and Italian vegetable soups renowned. What is a minestrone or a *soupe au pistou* but a splendid vegetable soup prepared with loving care and the freshest of vegetables, all in season.

Almost every country has its own version of what constitutes a vegetable soup or stock. Like meat stocks, vegetable stocks must be cooked slowly in order to extract all the mineral salts from the various vegetables used. Usually the vegetables are cut into small pieces to enable all their flavour to be extracted, and sautéed in oil or fat to improve flavour and food value.

As with meat stock, cold water is added, the whole brought to the boil, salt and pepper added, and the stock simmered until the vegetables are thoroughly cooked. The soup can be served as it is, puréed in a blender, or rubbed through a sieve. Strained, and the stock moderately clear, it can be used with other vegetables to make a soup of individual character, i.e. spinach, artichoke or tomato.

To thicken a vegetable soup (as with most other soups) use a roux, rather than a flour or cornflour and water paste; and, unless otherwise directed, add the stock to the roux and not the roux to the stock.

As with meat stocks, vegetable stocks can be clarified with egg whites, shells, tomatoes cut into pieces, and onion skins.

Most of the following recipes specify meat stock – which

does improve even a well-made vegetable soup, it must be admitted – but when this is not available, a bouillon cube may be used, or even water, although this is anathema to many cooks. Stock gives extra body and flavour, but to be honest it is not absolutely necessary for many vegetable soups.

A cheap but nevertheless good stock can be made with vegetable left-overs. Those outer leaves of cabbage (not the yellow and really ancient ones), lettuce and other greens, cauliflower stalks, carrot ends and peels, and those of turnips, parsnips and other root vegetables, can all be used. The peels and cores of tomatoes, skins of onions, ends of spring onions and leeks, the coarser stalks and leaves of celery, all can be boiled to make stock. If a bouillon cube or some meat stock is added, and the whole strained, this soup, with an interesting garnish, is good.

Almond soup

It is a curious fact that almond soup is one of *the* soups of Anglo-Indian cooking; it was served to Her Majesty Queen Elizabeth II on her Indian tour in Agra, the city of the Taj Mahal. It is a soup always to be found in cooking books of the last century, often dedicated to those 'English girls to whom Fate may assign the task of being house-mothers in our Eastern Empire'. Such books were somewhat anonymously written, the authors styling themselves 'An Anglo-Indian', or 'An Old Lady Resident'.

4 servings

225 gr (8 oz) blanched almonds
1·2 litres (2 pints) clear meat or chicken stock (white)
1 each clove, stick celery, leaf of mace, bay leaf and basil
salt, pepper
25–50 gr (1–2 oz) ham
sherry
whipped cream
slivers of blanched almonds as a garnish

Put the stock with the ham, herbs, celery, spices, salt and

pepper into a pan, bring gently to the boil, lower the heat and simmer for 30 minutes. Strain. Crush the almonds in a grinder or pound in a mortar (or let the blender do this tiresome job). Return the stock to the saucepan, add the almonds, stir well and simmer for another 15 minutes. Serve the soup hot, flavoured with a little sherry and garnished with slivers of almonds and tufts of whipped cream. If the almonds do not have sufficient flavour (and many do not these days), add just a suspicion of good quality almond flavouring. This is not a very thick soup but exceedingly pleasant.

Cream of chicken soup

4 servings

1·2 litres (2 pints) chicken stock
50 gr (2 oz) butter
50 gr (2 oz) flour
1 each onion, leek and stalk of celery, all chopped
chopped parsley
salt
2 egg yolks
1 cup slightly warmed cream

Heat the butter, add the flour and stir to a roux. Gradually add the stock, stirring all the while. Add the vegetables, parsley and salt, if required; lower the heat and simmer the soup for 30 minutes. Rub through a sieve or purée in a blender, then sift and return it to the pan. Bring to a gentle boil. Beat the yolks into the cream. Add this to the soup, whisking all the time. Let the soup come almost to the boil again and serve hot.

This simple but delicious soup is not expensive, as the stock can be made from chicken carcasses or by boiling a rather elderly bird which can be used as an entrée.

Burgundy hotpot (France)

12 or more servings

450 gr (1 lb) thick streaky bacon, rather fat
1 butt pork
1 salted knuckle pork
1 cabbage, cut in pieces
6 peeled, sliced carrots
6 peeled, sliced turnips
1 onion, stuck with 2 cloves
6 leeks, white parts only
2 cloves garlic
450 gr (1 lb) small or coarsely-chopped peeled potatoes
black bread
salt, pepper
3·5 litres (6 pints) water

Put the bacon and pork into a large saucepan or earthenware casserole. Add the unsalted water, bring to a gentle boil, lower the heat and cook for 2 hours or till the meat is quite tender. Skim fairly often. Take out the meat, skim the stock again and add the bracketed vegetables and garlic. Cover the pan and cook over a moderate heat for 1½ hours. Add the potatoes and cook these until soft. Test for seasoning – you will probably need pepper, but still no salt. Serve the soup and its vegetables and black bread. Slice the meats and serve these separately, preferably with a bottle of young white Burgundy.

When leeks are not available, very mild onions can replace them, but the flavour is by no means the same. When recipes say 'use only the white parts of the leeks', I either use the green parts in another recipe, or else ignore this bit of advice and use the lot. The above recipe makes a splendid supper party dish with not too much work for the housewife/cook. A green salad can be served with the meat.

Cheese soup (France)

This is another soup with no exact quantities. Have ready some meat or chicken stock or, better still, some thin onion soup. Toast – say – eight or ten slices of French bread and provide the same number of slices of Gruyère cheese; also grate a fair quantity. Arrange a layer of bread in the bottom of a soup tureen or a deep casserole. Cover this with a layer of cheese slices and grated cheese. Repeat this layering once or twice more, according to the size of the tureen; the top layer should be of cheese. Fill to brimming with stock or onion soup. Put into a moderate oven to let the cheese melt. Serve as a main course, to be followed by a salad or something extremely light.

The bread must be French, otherwise the result can be soggy. Although this soup is meant to be very substantial, do not have too many layers of bread. Left-over soup can be puréed in a blender, and enough chicken or meat stock added to make it into a first-class cheese soup of a more usual type. Recipes for this sort of soup vary throughout France. Some cooks use brown bread, and insist that the soup should be so thick that a spoon stands up in it. In some districts, only grated cheese is used. For those who prefer more liquid with their soups than this recipe gives, some boiling stock may be added to the plates when serving.

Chestnut soup

4 servings

900 gr (2 lb) chestnuts
50 gr (2 oz) butter
1·2 litres (2 pints) each chicken stock and milk
salt, pepper to taste
1 large, sliced peeled potato (optional)
a little chopped celery, leek and onion
1 clove garlic and 1 bay leaf
sugar
nutmeg
1·5 dl ($\frac{1}{4}$ pint) cream

To shell the chestnuts, make a gash in the side of each with a sharp knife. Plunge them into boiling water or into cold water brought to the boil, which is sometimes easier, and cook for 20 minutes. Drain the chestnuts and as soon as possible peel off inner and outer skins.

Put a few of the shelled chestnuts aside and leave these whole. Chop the remainder coarsely. Heat the butter, lightly fry the chopped chestnuts till golden, add the vegetables, garlic and bay leaf. When all the butter has been absorbed, add the stock and the milk and cook over a low heat till the chestnuts are soft. Rub the soup through a sieve – it should be as smooth as cream. If the soup is too thick, it can be diluted with more stock or milk. Return the soup to the pan, add salt, pepper, sugar and nutmeg. Immediately before serving, add the cream and garnish with the whole chestnuts. Alternatively, these can be used in the soup and a garnish of croûtons used. Two beaten egg yolks may be whisked into the cream.

This is a particularly delicious soup, but a word of warning is required. Some chestnuts are sweeter than others, so taste before adding sugar. Also, although most recipes for chestnuts give 20 minutes for their immersion in hot water, I have found chestnuts which require a far longer time. Some I have had in the hills of India have taken up to an hour before we were able to strip off the peels. However, this long cooking also softened the flesh within and they seemed to be unusually strong in flavour.

Apart from croûtons or whole chestnuts, diced and cooked game fillets may be used as a garnish. Instead of chicken stock, a dark beef stock may be used and a game, turkey or duck stock is especially recommended.

Garbure (France)

Garbure is a word of Spanish origin and means roughly the same as ragoût; indeed, the soup of this name so popular in areas of the Pyrenees could just as easily be classified as a ragoût. It would appear to be a Basque soup with a history of several centuries. There are many variations and imitations throughout France. Its origin, they say, is Béarnais and there the *garbure* is considered the 'jewel of the gastronomic crown'. Even in Béarn itself, *garbure* is variously prepared, but the variety is determined by the seasons. There are always, however, some essential ingredients; cabbage is one, beans, potatoes, pork or bacon are others. And, as with all such delicious peasant dishes, quantities are 'as required'. Like so many of these preparations, *garbure* tastes better the day after it has been cooked. It is so good that no one minds eating *garbure* two or three times running.

Choose a large casserole, preferably earthenware, of a fat and comfortable shape, and have ready fresh vegetables in season: carrots, turnips, onions, a good round and firm cabbage, haricot beans (or the French *mange-tout* peas), fresh white beans or, if not available, dried ones previously soaked overnight, and very young and small potatoes. These should weigh in all about four-and-a-half pounds. Then have ready a piece of salt pork or bacon (the recipe actually specifies Bayonne or Landes bacon).

Prepare all these vegetables and put them into the casserole with plenty of water. Bring it all to the boil, lower the heat and cook slowly for 3 hours. (If this can be achieved in the oven all the better.) After a couple of hours' cooking, test to see whether the pork or bacon is tender. If this is so, take it from the pan and put it aside. Continue cooking the *garbure*. When this is ready for eating, reheat the meat and cut it into thick slices. This is served separately.

In the meantime the soup should have become so thick that a soup ladle could stand up in it 'straight as a ninepin'. The *garbure* is served with a slice of bread in each plate or with croûtons and grated cheese.

As they finish their soup many people in the Béarn district add a glass of red wine to their bowls. This, complained Curnonsky, 'does not look very pretty at all, but the flavour is most agreeable'. Preserved duck is another ingredient added to the soup and is readily available in the Landes or Béarn area. Bacon rinds are a popular addition, and when tied together are easily removed. The remains of a goose, or garlic sausages, are other pleasant additions, and (to quote Curnonsky again) 'there are as many *garbures* as there are good chefs or Cordons Bleus'. Garlic, thyme and parsley are usual additions; when chestnuts are in season these are added and the potatoes omitted; but, if adding chestnuts, these must first be shelled and roasted.

Gravy or brown flour soup (Switzerland)

8 servings

5 tablespoonfuls butter
5 tablespoonfuls flour
2·5 litres (4 pints) clear stock
salt, pepper (if required)
grated Gruyère cheese
croûtons

Melt the butter, add the flour and stir to a brown roux. This must be done very slowly over a low heat till it is a chestnut colour. If too dark the soup becomes speckled, and if too light it has an unappetizing drab colour. Very slow cooking and continuous stirring produces an excellent colour and a delicious nutty flavour and aroma. It is well worth this trouble. When the roux is made, gradually add the stock, stirring all the while till a thick soup is produced. Let this cook gently for 1½ hours. Add salt and pepper just before serving. Serve with grated Gruyère cheese and croûtons.

This soup, rightly considered delicious by the Swiss, is served as a 'morning-after' dish and is offered to late-night revellers in Basel at carnival time when the entire population has been dancing all night in the streets, or at the close of big dances.

An old Bündner recipe says add 2 tablespoonfuls of red wine and a good pinch of salt as well as a coffeespoonful of sugar.

Jenny Lind soup

Jenny Lind was the 'Swedish Nightingale', and this soup was her invention or made in her honour. It is delicate in flavour, as well as being simple to prepare.

8 servings

75 gr (3 oz) sago
1·5 dl (¼ pint) cream
1·5 dl (¼ pint) milk
2 egg yolks
1 lump sugar
2·5 litres (4 pints) white stock
salt, pepper

Wash the sago in boiling water. Put the stock into a large saucepan, add the sugar, let it come almost to the boil, add the sago. Lower the heat and cook slowly for 30 minutes, Beat the egg yolks, add the milk and cream, stir them briskly into the soup and serve at once. Add salt and pepper to taste after testing. Do not let the soup boil.

Kidney soup (Holland)

6 servings

1 calf's kidney
1·8 litres (3 pints) meat stock
1 small, finely-chopped onion
50 gr (2 oz) butter
50 gr (2 oz) flour
250 ml (8 fl oz) light cream
2–3 tablespoonfuls Madeira

After removing the membrane from the kidney, halve it and remove the white veins and fat. Soak the halves in cold water for 2 hours, changing the water several times. Parboil the kidney in the stock for 15 minutes. Drain, keep the stock and dice the kidney. In the same pan heat the butter and cook the onion till tender. Sprinkle the flour over the top and blend it well into the butter. Add the stock and simmer for 15 minutes. Return the diced kidney to the pan and, when this is quite tender, add the cream; stir well, add the Madeira and serve the soup hot.

Liver soup (*Potage à l'Alsacienne*)

liver, heart and kidney of a goose
225 gr (½ lb) pig's liver
salt, pepper
dash of grated nutmeg
juice of 1 lemon
1 chopped onion and some chopped parsley
chicken or beef consommé or clear stock

Put all the ingredients except the consommé into a pan, add a little water and cook gently until the liver and kidney are soft. Rub through a sieve. Mix this purée with enough consommé to make a thinnish soup; reheat to serve, garnished with slightly salted whipped cream. Allow 3 dl (½ pint) of soup per serving.

Mushroom soup

4–6 servings

450 gr (1 lb) mushrooms
2 finely-chopped onions
75 gr (3 oz) butter
1·2 litres (2 pints) chicken stock
3 dl (½ pint) milk
50 gr (2 oz) flour
1·5 dl (¼ pint) cream
2 egg yolks
salt, pepper

Wash and chop the mushrooms. Melt the butter in a saucepan, add the onions and mushrooms and simmer for 10 minutes. Add the flour, blend into the mushrooms, add the stock, stirring all the while, and bring to the boil. Lower the heat and cook gently for 30 minutes, then add the milk. Strain through a sieve, or purée in a blender, and return to the pan. Mix the egg yolks with the cream, add this to the pan, bring almost to boiling point, add salt and pepper to taste, and serve hot.

To garnish, sauté 100 gr (4 oz) mushrooms in butter, add about half a cup of sherry, or a light sprinkling of paprika.

Mulligatawny (India)

By origin this is an Indian soup but it has been so 'worked upon' by successive generations of British housewives in India that it has lost its identity.

The word mulligatawny is a corruption of the Indian Tamil word *molegoo*, meaning pepper, and *tunee*, meaning water.

6–8 servings

1 boiling fowl or 900 gr (2 lb) breast of lamb
6 sliced onions
3 cloves garlic
3·5 litres (6 pints) water
1·25-cm (½-inch) piece green ginger (when possible, otherwise omit)
5-cm (2-inch) piece of cinnamon

6 tomatoes
1–2 bay leaves
a few coriander leaves, or English or Continental parsley
salt to taste
seasoning:
10 dried chillies
1 tablespoonful coriander seeds
½ tablespoonful cumin seeds
6 peppercorns
6 threads saffron soaked in water and pounded
2·5-cm (1-inch) piece of turmeric (this is what gives the soup its 'curry' flavour)
2·5-cm (1-inch) piece raw ginger (optional)
1½ breakfast cups of thick coconut, milk of almonds, cream or milk
1 finely-chopped onion
25 gr (1 oz) clarified butter

Joint the fowl or cut the mutton into small pieces. Put the pieces with the remaining ingredients except the seasonings into a large saucepan and cook gently till the meat is tender. Strain.

Pound the chillies, ginger, turmeric, peppercorns, seeds and saffron to a paste (the blender will also do this). Add the coconut cream.

Return 1·8 litres (3 pints) of the stock to the pan and add the spiced coconut liquid. Simmer the soup till it thickens slightly. Heat the butter and fry the onions lightly. Add these to the soup 5 minutes before serving.

Cooked rice and slices of lime or lemon are usually served as a garnish to this soup, as well as the meat cut into small pieces.

Some recipes suggest the addition of ground peanuts to make the soup thick. Others are slightly less prodigal in the amounts of seasoning boiled with the meat. The remains of the chicken or mutton may be used in other dishes, for the quantity of meat returned to the soup as a garnish is one's own affair.

It is interesting to read in Wyvern's *Culinary Jottings*, published in 1891, his comments on mulligatawny: 'If it must be admitted that the knack of curry-making has gradually passed away from the native cook, I think it must be allowed that a really well-made mulligatawny is comparatively speaking a thing of the past.' It should not be a thick soup but a *soupe maigre* or indeed 'pepper water'.

I think that the addition of a dessertspoonful of tamarind when making the chilli paste is excellent, and this is available at stores dealing with Eastern items of diet. The custom of adding rice to the soup is an old Anglo-Indian one, dating from the time when our forefathers in the Indian sub-continent served rice with everything they ate. (I am using the term Anglo-Indian in its old connotation, i.e. one who was English but lived and worked in India.)

For a clearer soup, instead of pounding the chillies, coriander seeds, etc., put them into a muslin bag and cook with the remaining ingredients. The flavour naturally is slightly less pronounced.

Oxtail soup (Germany)

6–8 servings

900 gr (2 lb) oxtail
100 gr (4 oz) lean ham or bacon, chopped
50 gr (2 oz) butter or dripping
2 each large onions and carrots, peeled and chopped
1 small head of celery or piece of celeriac
2·5 litres (4 pints) water
1 tablespoonful flour
1·5 dl (¼ pint) Burgundy or Madeira
good pinch of cayenne pepper
1 teaspoonful salt
¼ teaspoonful sugar

Wash the oxtail, season it well and cut into 5-cm (2-in) pieces. Heat the butter or dripping, add the bacon, the oxtail and vegetables and cook lightly till all are browned. Add the water, salt, pepper and sugar; bring the soup to the boil, lower the heat and simmer till the meat is tender. Strain. Mix the flour with enough water or milk to make a thin paste. Return the soup to the pan, bring to the boil, add the flour and water paste, cook, stirring all the time till it thickens. Take the meat from the bones, dice and return it to the pan. Add the wine, bring slowly to the boil and serve hot.

The Germans serve this soup either with hot toasted rolls, which is fine, or with macaroons. This latter is a specialized taste, but not mine. To the above ingredients can be added one or two bay leaves, a small piece of green ginger and a pinch of allspice. I do not think this soup requires further thickening.

Scotch broth

There's neeps intilt, and leeks intilt,
and parsley intilt. What's nae intilt?

4 servings

450 gr (1 lb) stewing beef or neck of mutton, with the fat trimmed off
1 carrot
1 turnip
50 gr (2 oz) split, dried whole or fresh peas
2 leeks
50–75 gr (2–3 oz) barley
salt, pepper
chopped parsley as a garnish

Peel the carrot and turnip and dice. Wash the leeks and split each into four. (If using dried peas, soak them overnight. If using fresh peas, add these about 10 minutes before the soup is ready.) Wash the barley. Wipe the meat and put into a pot with enough cold water for four people (about 1·2 litres or 2 pints). Add the barley and dried peas, if using. Bring this to the boil and skim. Add salt and pepper and continue to cook without boiling for 1 hour. Skim again, add the vegetables and continue to cook slowly till the meat is tender. When the broth is ready, the meat can be taken out and served like a *pot-au-feu* as a separate course. If not, cut into small pieces and return it to the soup as a garnish. The parsley is added at the very end of the cooking.

This soup will take 2–3 hours of cooking over a medium heat, so remember to add enough liquid to allow for evaporation.

Windsor cream soup

This is a light mock turtle soup garnished with crayfish *quenelles.*

Windsor soup

What a maligned soup – and what horrors the very name conjures up; and yet this soup is a very good one when made properly. Elizabeth Craig in her delightful cookery book *Court Favourites* (André Deutsch) gives its date as 1870, and her recipe adds *quenelles* of crayfish as a garnish.

8 servings

2·5 litres (4 pints) brown stock
50 gr (2 oz) butter
225 gr (½ lb) each shin of beef and mutton, cut into cubes
1 each large onion and carrot, peeled and sliced
50 gr (2 oz) flour
salt, pepper (preferably cayenne)
50 gr (2 oz) boiled rice (optional)
½–1 wineglass Madeira
bouquet garni

Heat the butter in a saucepan, add the meat and vegetables, and fry till brown. Sprinkle in the flour, stir and cook for 5 minutes. Add the stock, stirring all the while. Let the soup come to the boil, lower the heat and simmer with the bouquet garni till the meat is tender. Add salt and pepper, discard skin or bone of meat, and rub the soup through a sieve or, better still, purée in a blender. Return it to the pan, add the Madeira, reheat, add the rice (if using) and serve hot.

Velvet soup (*Potage à la Reine*)

4 servings

1 boiling fowl
salt, pepper
1 each chopped onion, stalk of celery, carrot and leek
bouquet garni
2 cloves
1·2 litres (2 pints) water
2 tablespoonfuls ground rice
3–4 egg yolks
1·5–3 dl (¼–½ pint) cream
25 gr (1 oz) butter

Put the fowl, salt and pepper, vegetables, bouquet garni and cloves with the water for the stock into a pan and bring to the boil. Lower the heat and simmer till the chicken is very tender. Strain the stock. Strip the flesh from the fowl, pound this in a mortar (or use a mincer or blender) and rub through a sieve. Mix the ground rice with some of the stock to make a thin paste. Stir this into the chicken purée, and then into the stock. Bring to the boil, stirring all the time, and cook for 5 minutes. Beat the egg yolk slightly, mix into the cream and stir this into the soup immediately before serving. Add the butter, blend this well and serve at once.

Vegetable soups

Vegetable stock

8 servings

900 gr (2 lb) mixed vegetables (carrots, leeks, onions, celery, turnips)
2·5 litres (4 pints) water
50 gr (2 oz) butter
salt, pepper, sugar to taste
mushrooms and peas as required
mixed herbs to taste (optional)

Chop all the vegetables finely. Heat the butter and fry the onions and leeks till they begin to brown, add the remainder of the vegetables, the seasonings and sugar and continue frying all these for a few minutes, then add several tablespoonfuls of water. Cover the pan and simmer till this becomes a glaze (this will make the soup clearer). Add the water, bring to the boil, skim, draw the pan to the side of the stove, add the mushrooms, herbs and peas, return to a low heat and simmer till all the vegetables are cooked (but not mushy); drain off the liquid. This stock may be used as it is, or clarified like other soups. Otherwise, instead of having a clear stock, the stock and vegetables can be rubbed through a sieve and served as a thick soup.

When possible, it is best to have more carrots in proportion to the other vegetables, and not too much turnip. Leeks may be omitted if they are out of season.

Black bean soup (USA)

Many Americans wax lyrical about this soup, which is a favourite Boston Sunday dish, one of those 'grandmother's' soups, and to some people one of the most delicious soups ever devised – an opinion with which I agree. It is described variously as being of Cuban or Mexican origin. It is not always easy to get black beans, but they should be available in speciality shops. I made an excellent imitation with black lentils. A similar soup can be made in exactly the same manner with dark red or brown beans. The result from the black beans is a soup of almost mahogany colour.

6–8 servings

450 gr (1 lb) black beans (these are a shiny black, roughly the size of haricot beans)
1 hambone, chuck of smoked pork, or rind of cooked smoked ham
2–3 sticks chopped celery
2–3 large chopped onions
2 tablespoonfuls butter
2 bay leaves
good handful of finely-chopped parsley
12 peppercorns
3 cloves
1 clove garlic
½ teaspoonful cayenne pepper
salt to taste
½ teaspoonful dried mustard
2·5 litres (4 pints) water
garnish:
thin slices lemon or lime
sliced hard-boiled eggs

Soak the beans overnight. Drain and put into a large saucepan with the salted water, the ham, bay leaves, parsley, cloves, celery, peppercorns and garlic. Bring this to the boil, lower the heat and simmer. Heat the butter and fry the onions gently until soft but not brown. Add these to the pan and finally add the cayenne pepper and mustard. Let all this cook gently till the beans are soft. Discard the bone and either purée the soup in a blender or rub it through a sieve. Return the purée to the pot, reheat and serve with the garnish.

Some recipes include a glass of Madeira or Marsala added to the soup before serving, also a scant cup of scalded cream. Another garnish is sliced raw onion and cooked pilau rice. Finely-chopped red or green peppers, cumin seed and finely-chopped fresh, or diced, oregano or marjoram are other alternatives.

Bean soup (Hungary)

5–6 servings

450 gr (1 lb) brown or red beans
75 gr (3 oz) lard or goose fat
1–2 large onions
2–3 tablespoonfuls flour
1–2 cloves garlic
1 tablespoonful paprika
salt to taste – but not too much
450 gr (1 lb) smoked pork or ham, chopped
3·5 litres (6 pints) water

Soak the beans for 12 hours, or as long as they take to soften. Next day put all the ingredients into a pan and cover. Simmer for as long as possible. One way is to put the soup into a large casserole and then leave it in the oven overnight – at any rate the soup needs simmering for at least 12 hours, and 24 is not too long. That is all.

Although this soup is one of the popular 'hangover', or so-called 'breakfast' soups, it does wonderfully as a main dish to be followed by something very light indeed.

White beans can be used in exactly the same manner.

Aubergine soup

6–8 servings

450 gr (1 lb) aubergine (eggplant)
6 tablespoonfuls oil, pork or chicken fat
4 peeled, chopped tomatoes
2 finely-chopped onions
1–2 minced cloves of garlic
1 crushed leaf basil and some fresh marjoram
1·8–2·5 litres (3–4 pints) clear meat stock or water
3 tablespoonfuls rice
salt, pepper
Parmesan cheese, grated

Peel the aubergine, cut into cubes (but not too thick). Heat the oil or fat, add the aubergine and fry this till the pieces are brown. Add the tomatoes, onion, herbs and garlic. Cook over a moderate heat till the mixture is soft. Add the stock, bring this to the boil and continue cooking till the vegetables are very soft. Stir frequently; 15 minutes before the soup is ready (it takes about 40 minutes altogether), add the rice and cook till this is soft. Add salt and pepper if required, serve hot, garnished with freshly-grated Parmesan cheese.

This soup is perhaps in the nature of being an accident; but it is a rich and splendid soup, with something of the flavour of Provence, or perhaps Italy.

Cabbage soup (Russia)

Whenever I make cabbage soup I am reminded of a fairly hilarious party in New Delhi with a group of foreign correspondents, including four Russians. One of the latter boasted that his wife could make the 'finest cabbage soup in the world'. In a moment of delicious champagne expansiveness, he invited my husband and me to sample this splendid soup. We accepted and arranged that the following day I should telephone to confirm. This I did. The wife answered the telephone, seemingly hale and hearty. Then came the husband to the phone. The champagne haze had worn off. I reminded him of his invitation (maybe it was unkind of me). There was a truly deathly silence, a sudden sigh: 'My wife,' he said, 'is ill.' I replied that I was sorry and hoped she would soon be better. Again a silence. Then, like a rush of forest wind, he said: 'I am sorry, but my wife is indefinitely ill.' To which there could be no reply.

My recipe for cabbage soup is, even so, Russian. But whether it competes with Madame X's soup, I shall never know: just how long is 'indefinitely'?

8 servings

2·5 litres (4 pints) meat stock
about 450 gr (1 lb) shredded white cabbage
2 each finely-chopped onions and carrots
finely-chopped celery or celeriac to taste
salt, pepper (to taste)
1·5 dl (¼ pint) sour cream
1 level tablespoonful flour
finely-chopped dill and parsley

Obviously the best stock for this soup is one of meat and bones, but, failing this, bouillon cubes can be used. Bring the stock to the boil in a large saucepan, add the carrots, celery and onions and cook for 15 minutes. Add the cabbage and continue cooking till this is tender. Take a little stock from the pan, mix this with the flour to a thin paste, and stir it into the cream. Pour this mixture slowly into the soup, stirring all the while, till it reaches boiling point. Immediately reduce the heat and simmer for a further 3 minutes. Sprinkle with dill and parsley just before serving.

For an even more filling soup, peeled chopped tomatoes and potatoes may be added.

In *The Forme of Cury*, published in 1390 on the authority of Richard II's highly qualified chief cook, we get this recipe for cabbage soup:

Caboches in pottage. Take caboches and quarter them in gode broth with onyons y-minced and the white of lekes y-slypt and corve (cut) smale, and do thereto safronn and salt and force it with powder douce (allspice).

French cauliflower soup (*Potage Dubarry*)

6–7 servings

2 small (or 1 very large) cauliflowers
1·8 litres (3 pints) white stock (preferably chicken but vegetable will do)
3 dl (½ pint) milk
3 dl (½ pint) cream
25 gr (1 oz) ground rice
salt, pepper to taste

Chop the cauliflower with the stalks and cook in salted water in the usual way till tender: drain and rub through a sieve, or purée in a blender. Keep the liquid. Mix the rice with enough milk to make a thin paste. Put the stock, the remainder of the milk and 6 dl (1 pint) of the cauliflower liquid into a pot. Bring all this to the boil, stir in the rice paste and, when blended, lower the heat and cook gently for 15 minutes. Add the cauliflower purée, the cream and the seasoning. Reheat without boiling. Serve with a sprinkling of chopped chervil, when available. If a slightly less thick soup is preferred, omit the ground rice.

Bortsch (Russia)

Bortsch ranks with the aristocrats of soup. It is the national soup of both Russia and Poland, and I do not intend here to enter into a discussion as to its origin. Sufficient to say that it is a symbol of the cooking of both these countries and that my recipe is from Moscow. But there are so many recipes and, although some gourmets are inclined to go into a ritual when making these bortsch soups, they are really extremely simple to prepare. Remember not to omit that dollop of sour cream, and then the soup can be tackled in the most approved Muscovite fashion.

6–8 servings

2·5 litres (4 pints) clear beef stock
1 hambone, weighing about 225 gr (½ lb)
450 gr (1 lb) raw beetroot
225 gr (½ lb) potatoes
450 gr (1 lb) cabbage
2 each carrots and onions
1 small parsnip (optional)
1 tablespoonful tomato purée
25 gr (1 oz) butter, oil or other fat
chopped parsley to taste
salt, pepper, sugar
1 tablespoonful vinegar
sour cream

Pour the stock into a large saucepan, add the bone and bring to a boil over a moderate heat. While this is cooking, wash, peel and grate the beetroot. Add these to the stock. Add the vinegar, bring the stock again to the boil, then put the pan on the side of the stove for 20 minutes, without heat.

Prepare the remaining vegetables. Wash and shred the cabbage, peel and chop the potatoes, carrots, parsnip and onions.

Heat the butter and fry the vegetables lightly. Add the tomato purée and stir well. Add salt, pepper and sugar. Transfer this mixture to the beetroot stock, bring it once to the boil, then cook slowly for about 40 minutes. Take out the hambone. If there is any edible meat on it, cut this into small pieces and return it to the soup. Add the parsley. (Small frankfurter-type sausages are often added to this kind of bortsch.) Before serving, pour into each soup plate one tablespoonful of sour cream.

Cream of artichoke or Palestine soup

The Jerusalem artichoke is not a true artichoke nor does it come from Jerusalem. It is a misshapen warty tuber and a nuisance to peel. It is, like the parsnip, one of those vegetables about which people have no half measures: either they like it immensely, or dislike it heartily. According to one of my culinary sources, Jerusalem artichokes are a species of sunflower native to the Americas and the name is a corruption of the Italian word *girasole*, which means 'turning to the sun'.

When making this soup it is not necessary to peel the artichokes first; simply cook them till very soft and rub through a sieve.

6–7 servings

900 gr (2 lb) Jerusalem artichokes
50 gr (2 oz) butter
2–3 thinly-sliced onions
1 stalk celery, chopped
1 clove
pinch of nutmeg
1·2 litres (2 pints) white stock
6 dl (1 pint) milk
a little shredded orange peel
salt, pepper
juice of 1 lemon

Wash and slice the artichokes. Put into a bowl with cold water and lemon juice to prevent discolouring. Heat the butter and fry the onions and celery. Simmer with the pan covered till these two ingredients are soft. Drain and dry the artichokes and add these to the onion and celery. Cook gently for 5 minutes. Add the stock, peel, clove and nutmeg, raise the heat and let the soup cook until the artichokes are soft. Rub through a sieve (or purée in a blender), return the soup to the pan, add milk, salt and pepper, and lemon juice and reheat and serve.

Alternatively, one may omit the milk and substitute 2 lightly-beaten egg yolks whisked into 3 dl (½ pint) cream. Stir this into the soup over a low heat for a few minutes. Do not allow the soup to boil. Serve with croûtons or diced, cooked chicken breasts; or, very simply, finely-chopped parsley.

Corn chowder (USA)

8–10 servings

100 gr (4 oz) diced salt pork
25 gr (1 oz) butter
2 each chopped onions, leeks and sticks celery
1·2 litres (2 pints) chicken stock
3 peeled and diced potatoes
2 cups corn, scraped from the cob
1·2 litres (2 pints) milk
salt, pepper
1·5 dl (¼ pint) cream
garnish:
50 gr (2 oz) butter
finely-chopped parsley

Put the pork into a large saucepan with the butter. When the fat has completely run from it, remove the crackling and put this aside; add the chopped vegetables to the pan and fry these until brown. Add the stock, bring this gently to the boil, add the potatoes and continue cooking till these are soft. Add the milk, bring the chowder again to the boil, add the corn, lower the heat and cook till the corn is soft – how long this will take depends on the corn, but good, young corn takes only a matter of 4–5 minutes. Add salt and pepper as required; immediately before serving, add the cream, garnish butter and parsley, and sprinkle into each bowl crumbled pork crackling. Serve hot.

Cream of asparagus soup

8–9 servings

1 bundle (450 gr or 1 lb) asparagus
50 gr (2 oz) butter
50 gr (2 oz) flour
1·8 litres (3 pints) white stock
6 dl (1 pint) milk
salt, pepper, ground nutmeg, sugar
1·5 dl (¼ pint) cream
mixed handful of cooked green peas and diced beans

Clean the asparagus and cut off the tips. Cook the latter carefully till soft and put aside for use as a garnish. Cut the stalks into small pieces, wash thoroughly in cold, salted water and boil in salted water until just tender. Drain. Heat the butter, add the flour, stir to a roux, gradually add the stock and milk, stirring all the while, bring to the boil, skim if necessary, and add the asparagus stalks, salt, pepper and nutmeg and a pinch of sugar. Cook gently till the stalks are very soft, rub this through a sieve, or purée in a blender, add more milk (if required) and bring again to the boil. Add the cream, stir this into the soup, add the peas, beans and asparagus tips and serve. A leaf of fresh borage may be added, or finely-chopped fresh tarragon or parsley. The soup may be served hot or cold; if served cold, add the cream after the soup is chilled.

Cream of green bean soup (Balkans)

4 servings

225 gr (½ lb) green or runner beans, preferably young and crisp
2 egg yolks
2 tablespoonfuls flour
1·5 dl (¼ pint) sour cream
1 teaspoonful lemon juice
1·2 litres (2 pints) water

Trim the beans and cook them whole in the boiling, salted water till tender but still crisp. Drain and keep the liquid. Chop the beans into 1·27-cm (half-inch) pieces. Return the liquid to the pot. Beat the yolks into the flour, add the sour cream (sour milk does equally well) and the lemon juice. Stir this into the simmering soup and continue stirring until it is thick and smooth. Add the beans and continue cooking until reheated.

Cream of beetroot soup

6 servings

2–3 beetroots
1 peeled and sliced onion
stalks of chopped celery, to taste
1·8 litres (3 pints) strained meat stock or water
50 gr (2 oz) butter
50 gr (2 oz) flour
1·5 dl (¼ pint) cream
salt, pepper

Cook the beetroots in the stock till soft; drain, peel and grate them. Heat the butter, add the onion and celery and cook this gently till soft. Sprinkle in the flour and stir till the mixture is blended. Add the stock and cook, stirring all the while, till the mixture thickens. Add the grated beetroot, salt and pepper, lower the heat and continue cooking for another 15 minutes.

Rub the soup through a sieve, return it to the pan, add the cream, reheat without boiling and serve hot.

Garnish the soup with whipped fresh or sour cream, chopped herbs, caraway seeds, fried croûtons or mustard and cress.

Cream of broccoli soup

8–9 servings

1 stalk celery, 1 small onion, 1 paprika pepper (all finely chopped)
25 gr (1 oz) butter
900 gr (2 lb) broccoli
25 gr (1 oz) flour
1·5–2·5 litres (3–4 pints) chicken stock
1–2 egg yolks
1·5 dl (¼ pint) cream
salt, pepper
(note: discard the seeds and core of the paprika pepper)
garnish:
a few of the best broccoli flowerlets
unsweetened whipped cream

Cook the broccoli with the remaining vegetables in salted, boiling water till tender. Drain, keep the liquid and reserve some flowerlets for a garnish.

In the same saucepan, heat the butter, add the flour and stir until blended. Gradually add the chicken and broccoli stock and stir till the mixture is thick. Add the broccoli (not the garnish) and other vegetables. Simmer this mixture for 20 minutes, rub it through a sieve and return it to the pan. Beat the egg yolks, whisk these into the cream and stir these into the soup. Reheat but do not let the soup come again to the boil. Add salt and pepper and serve hot, with the garnish.

Another method is to cream all the broccoli and garnish the soup with thin slices of lemon, chopped chives or chervil, or with a garnish of thinly-sliced spring onions, or chives and sour cream.

Cream of celery soup

6 servings

1 whole head celery
1 small chopped onion
50 gr (2 oz) butter
1·2 litres (2 pints) good white stock
6 dl (1 pint) milk
1·5 dl (¼ pint) cream
salt, pepper
croûtons

Wash the celery, trim and cut it into small pieces, including the leaves. Heat the butter in a saucepan, add the celery and onion and cook for 10 minutes. Add the stock and half the milk and continue cooking until the celery is very soft. Rub this through a sieve, or purée in a blender. Return it to the pot, add salt and pepper, the remainder of the milk and the cream. Reheat without allowing to boil. Diced carrots can be added, also a pinch of fresh thyme and a bay leaf. Add nutmeg or balls of Roquefort flavoured with finely-chopped parsley. Serve hot with croûtons.

Cream of parsley soup

4 servings

1 large bunch fresh parsley, finely chopped
9 dl (1½ pints) clear chicken broth
salt, pepper to taste
6 dl (1 pint) cream
2 egg yolks

Bring the stock to the boil, add the parsley, lower the heat and cook for about 30 minutes. Beat the yolks, stir these into the cream, add this mixture to the soup, and stir over a very low heat till the soup thickens slightly. Do not let it boil. Add seasoning and serve hot with croûtons.

This soup can also be served iced, garnished with whipped cream.

Cucumber soup

4 servings

2–3 cucumbers, according to size
75 gr (3 oz) butter
1·2 litres (2 pints) white stock or water
2 minced onions
handful minced parsley and celery leaves
salt, pepper and sugar
1·5–3 dl (¼–½ pint) cream
1 teacupful soft white breadcrumbs
milk

Soak the breadcrumbs in a little milk and squeeze them dry. Peel the cucumbers and cut them into small pieces; parboil in salted water. Drain. Heat the butter, simmer the cucumbers till soft; add the stock, stir this thoroughly, add the breadcrumbs, onions, parsley and celery leaves, salt, pepper and 1 teaspoonful sugar. Bring to the boil, lower the heat and simmer for 30 minutes, stirring from time to time. Rub through a sieve, or purée in a blender. If the soup is too thick, dilute it with a little milk or stock. If serving the soup hot, add the cream just before serving. If cold, let the soup cool before adding the cream, then chill.

Sprinkle each serving with finely-chopped chives, borage, fresh tarragon, dill, diced paprikas or croûtons.

Cream of carrot soup (*Purée Crécy*)

8 servings

- 450 gr (1 lb) thinly-peeled or scraped carrots
- 1 large peeled onion
- 1 large peeled turnip
- 1 leek, when available
- 50 gr (2 oz) butter, pork fat or dripping
- 2·5 litres (4 pints) hot water or vegetable stock
- salt, pepper
- 2 lumps sugar
- 6 bacon rinds
- 25 gr (1 oz) butter
- croûtons
- finely-chopped dill or parsley

Chop the vegetables coarsely. Heat the first quantity of fat or butter, add the vegetables and simmer these till soft. Gradually add the liquid, salt, pepper, sugar and bacon rinds. Continue cooking till the stock is boiling and the carrots soft, Rub the soup through a sieve back into the pan. Add the second quantity of butter, stir and serve with croûtons, parsley and dill, or cooked pilau rice.

The French call this soup Crécy because their best carrots grow in the town of this name.

Cream of lettuce soup

6 servings

- 2 heads lettuce (the greener the better)
- 6 dl (1 pint) slightly salted water
- 1·2 litres (2 pints) milk
- a little sliced onion and some parsley
- 1 clove and 1 bay leaf
- 37 gr (1½ oz) butter
- 25 gr (1 oz) flour
- salt, pepper, dash of nutmeg
- 2 beaten egg yolks
- 1·5–3 dl (¼–½ pint) thin cream or top of the milk
- a small knob of unsalted butter as a garnish

Wash the lettuce, break off the leaves, discard any which are wilted. Shred the good leaves finely, wash them again, drain and dry in a towel. Bring the water to the boil, drop in the shredded lettuce, and blanch for 5 minutes. Drain. Over a low heat scald the milk with the onion, parsley, clove and bay leaf. Strain.

Heat the butter, add the flour, stir to a roux and gradually pour the milk into this, stirring all the while. Cook over a low heat, still stirring, till the mixture thickens and boils gently. Add the lettuce and continue very slow cooking, stirring from time to time, for about 30 minutes. Add salt, pepper and nutmeg, rub the soup through a fine sieve (or purée in a blender), reheat, bringing it just to the boil. Stir the yolks into the cream, add this to the soup, whisk, and when blended add the garnish butter, stir again and serve hot. Garnish with chopped chervil or parsley and, of course, croûtons.

Lentil soup

6 servings

450 gr (1 lb) lentils
1 hambone, preferably without too much fat
2–3 peeled, coarsely-chopped carrots
1–2 large coarsely-chopped onions
a good handful of celery leaves, when available
1 bay leaf
2 peeled, chopped cloves garlic
about 1·2 litres (2 pints) water
1 cup of the top of the milk or thin cream
salt and pepper to taste
garnishes:
diced ham, grated cheese or fried onions

Wash the lentils thoroughly and put them into a large saucepan. Add the hambone, vegetables, bay leaf, garlic and water. Bring gently to the boil, lower the heat and simmer till the lentils and vegetables are soft. Take out the hambone, put this aside, skim off any excess fat and rub the soup through a fine sieve. Return the soup to the pan, add salt and pepper to taste. Bring it to the boil, add milk or cream, let this come just to the boil, remove and serve hot.

This is an excellent soup and a meal in itself. A little more water may be added if the soup, after sieving, proves too thick. Another recipe I have adds about 450 gr (1 lb) of peeled and cooked tomatoes to the soup just before adding the milk.

If there is any edible meat on the hambone, cut this into dice and return it to the pan with the sieved soup. Grated cheese may be served with this soup and a large bowl piled with crisply-fried onions.

In Iran one tablespoonful of dried mint is mixed with a quarter of a teaspoonful each of ground cinnamon and black pepper. This mixture is sprinkled over the soup just before serving. Sliced frankfurters may be dropped into the soup at the same time.

Fennel soup (Sicily)

I discovered this soup for the first time in Sicily, but similar soups are made wherever fennel abounds. Sicilians, it seems to me, are ready to eat fennel with almost everything. They have a fondness for the wild variety, collecting its tiny leaves and boiling them to make sauce for a pasta.

The variety of fennel used in this recipe is peculiar to Sicily, although the Florentine fennel may be used in precisely the same manner. Fennel has a large, bulbous root like an overgrown celery head and can be used in most of the ways in which we use celery or celeriac. Fennel is available, as far as I know, almost all of the time in Sicily, but its main season is winter and early spring. Truckloads of it go into the markets and shops. Fennel has the rich flavour of aniseed and, for the *aficionada*, is one of the most delicious of vegetables.

Separate the stalks of one or two heads of fennel and slice

them. Put into a saucepan with as much stock as required, bring to a slow boil and cook gently till the fennel is soft. Strain and rub through a sieve, or purée in a blender. Return the soup to the pan, measure it as you do so. Bring it to the boil. Make an egg and lemon sauce, using 1 egg yolk and 1 tablespoonful of lemon juice to each pint of stock. Mix the yolks with the lemon juice and mix this into half a cupful of hot stock. Beat this well and turn it into the soup, stirring all the while. Reheat almost to boiling point, take the pan from the heat and leave for 5 minutes before serving.

This is a marriage between Sicilian and Greek cooking, which is not unusual as the Greeks had a hand in the turbulent Sicilian past.

Parsnip soup

5–6 servings

450 gr (1 lb) parsnips
2 leeks (when in season, otherwise a mild onion)
3 dl (½ pint) cream or top of the milk
1·5 dl (¼ pint) white wine
salt, cayenne pepper (to taste)
croûtons
1·8 litres (3 pints) chicken stock

Scrape and chop the parsnips. Clean and slice the leeks or onion. Put all into a pan with enough water to cover and cook until very soft. Purée in a blender, or rub through a sieve. Mix the purée with the stock, add seasoning to taste, and return the soup to the pan. Bring just to boiling point, then add the cream and wine. Serve with croûtons.

Watercress can be served as a garnish. As this soup is rather sweet, the flavour is improved by the addition of either Tabasco or Jamaican pepper wine (*see* page 28).

Sweet pepper soup (USA)

5–6 servings

450 gr (1 lb) green or red sweet peppers
1 each large, finely-chopped onion and tomato
75 gr (3 oz) butter
37 gr (1½ oz) flour
1·8 litres (3 pints) clear stock or water
3 dl (½ pint) milk
salt, pepper, sugar (to taste)

Cut off the tops of the peppers, take out the core and seeds. (Do not lick your fingers after this operation: those seeds are hot.) Chop the peppers fine. Put aside one tablespoonful for a garnish. Heat half the butter in a saucepan, add the onion and cook it till soft and golden. Do not let it brown. Add the tomato, peppers and stock (or water) and cook the mixture gently till the peppers are soft. Rub through a sieve or, better still, purée in a blender. In the same pan, heat the remaining butter and stir in the flour to make a roux. Gradually add the milk, stirring till the mixture is thick. Return the pepper purée to the pan, stirring all the while. Simmer to reheat the soup, add salt, pepper and sugar. Continue cooking for a further 10 minutes. Serve sprinkled with chopped pepper, or very crisply fried chopped bacon, or both.

Spinach soup

5–6 servings

900 gr (2 lb) fresh spinach
1 finely-chopped onion
50 gr (2 oz) butter
37 gr (1½ oz) flour
1·2 litres (2 pints) stock
1·5 dl (¼ pint) cream
salt, cayenne pepper, grated nutmeg

Pick the spinach leaves from the stalks and wash them till quite free from dirt and grit. Heat the butter, add the onion, let this simmer a while, add the flour, stir and cook till it starts to get golden. Add the spinach, stir for a few minutes, gradually add the stock and cook gently till the spinach is tender. Rub through a fine sieve, or purée in a blender. Return the soup to the pan, dilute with more stock, if required; add salt, cayenne pepper and nutmeg to taste. If the colour is not good, add a little green vegetable colouring. Add the cream, stir this into the soup, reheat and serve.

There are several garnishes which marry with this soup. Whipped cream and finely-chopped parsley; plain or garlic-flavoured croûtons; diced, crisply-fried bacon; tufts of creamed liver pâté; a film of paprika, and Melba toast floating on the top of the soup.

When eggs are plentiful and cheap, 2 or 3 may be whisked into the cream before adding this to the soup, or the quantity of the cream may be doubled. Parsley and thyme may also be cooked with the spinach as well as finely-chopped celery leaves, chopped carrot and turnip.

Minestrone alla Milanese (Italy)

8 servings

225 gr (8 oz) dried beans
2 potatoes
2 tomatoes
2 courgettes
2 peeled, chopped carrots
½ small, chopped cabbage
1 stalk of celery and 1 onion, chopped
handful of fresh peas
1 chopped clove garlic
100 gr (4 oz) rice
50 gr (2 oz) cooking fat or oil
2·5 litres (4 pints) hot water
25 gr (1 oz) butter
2–3 bacon rinds
grated Parmesan cheese
salt, pepper, pinch of sage

Soak the beans overnight and stew until tender. Peel and chop the potatoes, tomatoes and courgettes. Heat the fat and the butter together, add the bacon rinds and fry till crisp. Take out the rinds, add the vegetables, including the garlic, and fry lightly. Add the water to the pan, bring slowly to the boil, add the rice and beans and continue boiling for 15 minutes. Add salt, pepper and sage. Sprinkle the soup generously with cheese, stir well and serve hot.

Instead of water, a thin second stock may be used; also sliced smoked Milanese sausages may be added, and a few asparagus tips.

Potato soup (*Potage Parmentier*)

6 servings

2–3 leeks, white parts only, finely chopped
50 gr (2 oz) butter
900 gr (2 lb) potatoes, peeled and chopped
9 dl (1½ pints) water or vegetable stock
salt, pepper
milk
1–2 egg yolks
1·5 dl (¼ pint) cream (more if preferred)
croûtons, or finely-chopped dill or chives as a garnish

Heat the butter, add the leeks and simmer these till soft, but not brown. Add the potatoes, then the liquid, salt and pepper, and cook this till the potatoes are soft. Rub through a sieve, return the soup to the pot, add enough milk to thin the soup to the required consistency. Bring this gently to the boil. Beat the egg yolks, whisk them into the cream and then into the hot soup. Do not let the soup boil. Serve hot, garnished with finely-chopped green herbs.

Onions may be used instead of leeks which, of course, changes the flavour, but even so produces a good soup.

Pea soup

4 servings

450 gr (1 lb) shelled peas
1 small lettuce, a little fresh mint and parsley
1 teaspoonful sugar
½ cucumber
1 medium-sized onion (or 6 spring onions)
50 gr (2 oz) butter
1·2 litres (2 pints) stock, preferably chicken
1·5 dl (¼ pint) milk
1·5 dl (¼ pint) cream or all cream
salt, pepper

Peel and chop finely the cucumber and onion; clean and chop

the lettuce, mint and parsley. Heat the butter in a large saucepan. Add the lettuce, cucumber, onion and herbs and stir them as they cook till all the butter is absorbed. Add salt, pepper and sugar, the peas and the stock. Bring to the boil, lower the heat and cook the peas gently till very soft. Rub through a sieve, or purée in a blender, correct seasoning, add the milk and the cream, gently reheat (but do not boil) and serve hot.

There are many suitable garnishes for this soup. Plain or garlic-flavoured croûtons; finely-chopped chervil; strips of hard-boiled egg whites; diced, peeled and seeded tomatoes, or green peppers. Instead of stirring the cream into the soup, each portion can be topped with a tuft of whipped cream.

For *Potage Gounod* add a garnish of *julienne* strips of chicken breasts. Chopped sorrel or spinach may be used instead of lettuce. This soup generally is served iced. After making the purée, let the soup become very cold, add the cream and flavour with sherry and then put into the refrigerator till iced.

Pea-pod soup

A thrifty soup but extremely good; however, it should only be made with pods which are garden fresh and tender, as they are then at their best.

6 servings

900 gr (2 lb) pea pods
1 good-sized lettuce, washed and broken apart
1 large handful chopped parsley
1 large, chopped onion
1·8 litres (3 pints) water or chicken stock
salt, pepper
1 teaspoonful sugar
25 gr (1 oz) butter
1 tablespoonful flour
1·5–3 dl (¼–½ pint) cream
croûtons

Wash the pods, trim them (i.e. strip off the stems and any strings) and put into a saucepan with the lettuce, parsley and onion. Add the liquid, salt, pepper and sugar, bring to the boil, lower the heat and cook till the pods are very soft. Either strain through a sieve (which means much forcing) or purée it all in a blender, then rub through a sieve. Heat the butter; in the same pan stir in the flour and, when blended, gradually add the soup, stirring all the while till it is thick and smooth. Bring it to the boil, lower the heat, add the cream, stirring constantly till reheated. Serve hot with croûtons or finely-chopped parsley, or any of the pea-soup garnishes.

Not being strong in the arm, I treat this only as a blender soup, although the *mouli* grater, which sometimes tries my patience, works admirably. The soup is smooth, of a delicate colour and full flavoured.

White bean soup (*Soupe au Pistou*) (France)

This hails from the Mediterranean where it is the early summer soup *par excellence*. It should be made from fresh white beans, broad beans and basil. In the market, vendors will call as you pass: '*Mesdames, faites le bon piste, faites le pistou.*' The *pistou*, like the Italian *pesto*, is a garlic sauce with plenty of finely-chopped fresh basil, olive oil and tomato. Although fresh white beans are traditional, the soup may be made with dried and soaked beans, with runner beans, fresh or frozen. When fresh basil is not available, use dried.

12 servings

3·5 litres (6 pints) water
450 gr (1 lb) each peeled potatoes, white beans and tomatoes
onions to taste and, when available, chopped white of leeks
salt – a goodly quantity of this
225 gr (½ lb) vermicelli or other pasta such as shells
5 cloves garlic
4 tablespoonfuls finely-chopped fresh basil (1 tablespoonful dried)
2 tablespoonfuls olive oil
4 tablespoonfuls tomato paste

Put the water, plenty of salt, the potatoes, beans, tomatoes, onions and leeks into a large pan. Bring to the boil, lower the heat and simmer for 30 minutes, or till the vegetables are cooked. Add the vermicelli or chosen pasta and continue cooking till this is soft. Stir frequently. In the meantime prepare the *pistou.* Pound the garlic to a paste, add the basil and the oil (drop by drop) and about 4 tablespoonfuls of tomato paste or fresh tomato juice. When the soup is ready, add this sauce, stirring it in gradually. Add, or serve, grated Gruyère cheese. If using dried, soaked white beans, cook these till almost tender before adding the other vegetables to the pan.

There are variations to this soup, which is a kind of minestrone. Chopped runner beans may be added; less of the pasta; medium-sized *courgettes*; or try chopped celery leaves. It simply does not matter as long as the '*pistou, le bon pistou*' is there acting as a transformer.

I found this *bon pistou* could also be added with great advantage to other thick vegetable soups. The quantity of basil may seem startling, but it is definitely not too much for the herb lover.

Purée Duboys (France)

6–8 servings

(Use a measuring cup)
1 cup white beans (soaked overnight)
1 cup lentils
1 each large peeled, sliced carrot and potato
1 teaspoonful tapioca or sago per person
a good handful chopped sorrel or watercress
salt, pepper, butter
wine vinegar

Put a large saucepan full of cold water on to the fire, add the lentils and beans and cook them till soft. Add salt and pepper. Heat about 1 tablespoonful of butter, add the chopped sorrel and let this simmer. Meanwhile add the tapioca, carrot and potato to the beans, etc., and when these are cooked, add the sorrel. Stir, rub through a sieve or purée in a blender. Return everything to the saucepan, add a little wine vinegar (if the sorrel has not sharpened the soup sufficiently), test for seasoning, serve sprinkled lightly with chopped herbs. This is an excellent soup, deserving of the tureen treatment.

Tomato and cheese soup (Switzerland)

5–6 servings

900 gr (2 lb) tomatoes, or 1 large tin tomato purée
1 large onion, finely chopped
1 clove garlic, finely chopped
1 tablespoonful flour
1 tablespoonful olive oil
salt, pepper, sugar, rosemary
3 dl (½ pint) thick cream
1 egg yolk
1·5 litres (2½ pints) water
225 gr (8 oz) grated Swiss cheese

Chop the tomatoes fine if fresh ones are being used. Heat the oil, add the onion and garlic and tomatoes or purée. Let them all cook for a few minutes, then stir in the flour. When blended, add the water, stirring all the while. Let this mixture simmer for about 30 minutes, or till the tomatoes are quite soft. Rub all this through a sieve and return to the pan. Add seasoning, sugar and rosemary. Mix the cream with the egg yolk, take a little of the tomato soup and mix it well into the cream and egg mixture. When the soup is reheated, quickly add the cream and egg mixture and whisk it briskly all the while, but never bring to the boil. Serve with a generous amount of cheese.

This soup can also be garnished with chopped chives, sour or fresh cream, croûtons and, of course, other finely-chopped green herbs. It changes its character, naturally, but the basic flavour remains tomato.

Lentil soup (Arab style)

6 servings

450 gr (1 lb) breast of lamb or mutton
450 gr (1 lb) lentils
1 large, finely-chopped onion
2–4 cloves garlic
½ teaspoonful each turmeric and black pepper
½ cup strained lemon or lime juice
2·5 litres (4 pints) hot water
½ small, hard cabbage, finely chopped
1 heaped teaspoonful salt
garnish:
sliced raw onions, radishes and chopped mint

Put the meat and the lentils into a large saucepan. Add the onion, garlic, spices, lemon juice and water. Cover tightly and cook over a low heat for 1½ hours. Add the cabbage and salt. Cover again and continue cooking slowly for another hour, or till the meat is tender. If required, more water may be added from time to time. Strain off the liquid and serve this separately as a soup. Take out the meat and cut this into cubes. Mash the lentils and form into a mound on a plate; garnish with the meat, radishes, sliced onions, mint and sliced fried onions and surround the mound with baked tomatoes. Or garnish with croûtons or dough peas (*see* pages 29–31).

Turnip soup (*Purée Nivernaise*)

10 servings

2·5 litres (4 pints) white stock
900 gr (2 lb) turnips
450 gr (1 lb) potatoes
2–3 leeks
salt, pepper, nutmeg (to taste)
3 dl (½ pint) cream
50 gr (2 oz) butter

Wash and peel the turnips and potatoes, then slice thinly. Wash the leeks, trim off the root and green part (I use as much of this as possible) and slice thinly. Heat the butter, add the vegetables, and simmer for about 20 minutes, stirring occasionally. Add the stock, salt, pepper and nutmeg. Cook gently till all the vegetables are very soft. Rub through a sieve, or purée in a blender, return to the pan, add the cream and let the soup become hot (but not boiling). Serve hot.

Suggested garnishes for the soup are cooked and lightly-fried Brussels sprouts and diced, cooked, mixed vegetables, croûtons or finely-chopped parsley.

Watercress soup (1) (France)

5–6 servings

3–4 bundles watercress, depending on size and quality
50 gr (2 oz) butter
25 gr (1 oz) flour
1·8 litres (3 pints) boiling chicken stock or water
2–3 tablespoonfuls rice
1 egg yolk
salt, pepper

Wash the watercress, reserve some of the best leaves for a garnish, and chop the remainder finely. Heat the butter, add the watercress and cook for 10 minutes. Sprinkle in the flour, stir well, and gradually add the stock, or water, stirring all the time to keep the mixture smooth. Cook gently for 15 minutes. Bring the soup to the boil, add the rice and cook till this is soft. Add salt and pepper.

Take a little of the liquid and beat this gradually into the egg yolk. Stir it back into the soup immediately before serving. Add reserved cress and serve hot.

Watercress soup (2)

5–6 servings

3 bundles watercress, treated as above
6 finely-chopped spring onions
50 gr (2 oz) butter
salt, pepper
37 gr (1½ oz) flour
1·8 litres (3 pints) boiling chicken stock
2 egg yolks
3 dl (½ pint) cream
small knob butter

Heat the butter, add the spring onions and cook, covered, over a moderate heat till they are soft but not brown. Add the watercress and salt, cover the pan again and cook gently for about 5 minutes, or till the leaves are soft. Sprinkle in the flour, stir the mixture well and cook over a moderate heat for about 3 minutes. Gradually stir the stock into the watercress, cook for a few minutes, then rub through a sieve, a *mouli* grater, or purée in a blender. Return the purée to the pan. Heat to simmering.

Beat the egg yolks and blend with the cream. Gradually add this to the soup, being careful not to bring the soup to the boil. Add the butter and stir this into the soup. Serve hot, garnished with the reserved watercress leaves.

This soup may be served iced, in which case omit the final knob of butter.

To make *Potage à l'Oseille*, a famous French soup, substitute sorrel for watercress.

Vichyssoise soup

This exceedingly popular soup, generally thought of as American, is simply a refinement of a French potato and leek soup. It can be very good but unhappily, owing to its popularity, it has become somewhat debased. It must be absolutely chilled and to procure the real flavour it *must* be prepared with leeks, and they must be very white ones.

4–5 servings

4 good-sized leeks
1 medium-sized onion
50 gr (2 oz) butter
6 medium-sized potatoes
1·2 litres (2 pints) chicken stock
salt, white pepper
6 dl (1 pint) scalded milk
6 dl (1 pint) single cream
3 dl (½ pint) double cream

Wash the leeks and slice the white parts finely (reserve the green parts for flavouring in other soups). Peel and chop the onion. Heat the butter, add the leeks and onion, and cook gently till soft but keeping them white. Add the chicken stock and chopped potatoes and cook till tender. Add salt and pepper to taste and rub through a sieve, or purée in a blender and then rub through a sieve. Return the soup to the pan, add the milk, stir this well into the soup, then add the single cream, still stirring. Bring the mixture to the boil, add more salt and pepper if required, take from the heat and cool. When cool, add double cream and chill thoroughly. Serve with chopped chives.

This soup may well be made 24 hours in advance. As 'German sausage' during the First World War became 'breakfast sausage', so this soup was given a new name during the Second World War. It became *Crème* (or Soup) *Gaulloise*. But, unlike German sausage, the soup has reverted to its erstwhile name. A variation on the Vichyssoise theme is to blend iced tomato juice into the soup, about one quarter cup to every cup of Vichyssoise.

Onion soups

Such savoury deities must sure be good
Which serve at once for worship and for food.
(Juvenal)

This is at once a reference to the onion's adaptability in the kitchen and its worship by the ancient Egyptians as a god; for to these ancients, the onion *was* a god, as well as a staple item of diet. They swore by the gods and by the onion.

Onions, which most likely originated on the shores of the Mediterranean or southern Asia, have been esteemed since earliest recorded times. Travellers used them as a thirst preventative and soldiers munched them on long marches.

Onions, leeks, chives, garlic and shallots are all members of the same family, but the onion is the head of the family, and onion soup one of the most popular methods of dealing with it.

In France, onion soups have a special meaning; they are sometimes called the *soupe d'ivrogne*, and it is claimed they possess great powers of curing when it comes to dealing with alcoholic over-indulgence. Our mothers, and our grandmothers before them, believed that the onion, as a soup or a sauce, whole or even raw, could work wonders for the common cold.

There are several varieties of the onion and, say the pundits, one should use the right onion for the right job. This is all very well, but nowadays we often have to take what we can get. However, the rules are worth remembering. The larger the onion, the warmer its climate, the milder the flavour. As climates become sterner, so the onion becomes hardier and stronger flavoured and also keeps better. Where onions can be grown all the year round, they tend to be of poor quality.

Colours vary through white, yellow to a purple-red. The colour is also an indication of flavour. White onions are usually milder than either red or yellow, and are better for making creamed onion soups and sauces.

When cooking onions it is wise to have a chopping board for use of the onion family only. Another asset is a small, sharp knife, or the continental crescent-shaped chopper, which I value highly. Cutting is a problem and I have not yet discovered the perfect onion mincing or cutting gadget. It helps when cutting the peeled onion to slice it through at right angles, making a checker board, and then cut across. The small dice will fall out fairly easily.

Then there is the vexed question of onion tears, far worse than any crocodile's. Some declare that peeling and cutting the onion under running water helps. If peeling a fair number, put them into hot water for a minute or so; this helps to remove the skins also. But with all this I still find that tears live in an onion.

Finally there is the problem of the smell on one's hands after dealing with this flavoursome nuisance. Wash the hands in cold water. If this is not successful, make a paste of soda, flour and water and rub this well into the hands, washing it off in cold water. If this is too much bother, dry mustard rubbed into the hands will also help to remove onion odour.

If there is one soup universally popular, it is onion soup, in homes and in restaurants. Cooks, both professional and amateur, take pride in their onion soups and, as there are many different types to choose from, all can happily claim to have a really authentic recipe.

Unfortunately, onion soup is not always as good as it should be. It must not be a pallid liquid in which float limp specks of dark onion and a minute sprinkling of grated cheese. Made with proper care, onion soup is neither difficult nor expensive to prepare. Perhaps the most important point is that it should be neither bitter nor too harsh in flavour, but a smooth, pungent and often golden concoction.

Onion Soup (France)

6–8 servings

6–8 large onions
75 gr (3 oz) butter
salt, pepper
½ teaspoonful sugar
25 gr (1 oz) flour
1·8–2·5 litres (3–4 pints) chicken stock
garnish:
toasted French bread and grated Gruyère cheese

Peel the onions and slice them thinly. Heat the butter, add the onions, cover the pan and simmer over a low heat till these are soft. Add salt, pepper and sugar. Sprinkle in the flour, blend it well, and cook for 2–3 minutes, stirring all the time. Add the stock gradually, still stirring. When finally blended, cover the pan again and cook slowly for 30 minutes. Serve hot. In each portion put a slice of toast generously sprinkled with cheese.

A glass of dry white wine may be added to the soup before serving.

Water and salt soup (*Agua y Sal*) (Spain)

Surely there cannot be a more simple soup than this. It has no rules, or indeed any quantities, since they are 'as required' in the truest sense. It is a simple peasant soup, but one which even the most affluent need not despise. It can be varied, be made richer or poorer.

Take as many sliced onions as required and simmer them in olive oil, with chopped parsley, plenty of salt and pepper, till they are soft but not brown. Add water – about 3 dl (½ pint) for each person. Cook over a moderate heat till the onions are soft. Or the soup may be put into a blender and returned to the pan to reheat. Serve the soup hot, each portion topped with a poached egg.

About 900 gr (2 lb) onions makes enough soup for between six and eight people. I think it makes for easier eating if the onions are finely chopped, as slices will run off the spoon back into the plate.

These soups are extremely popular in Spain, also in Spanish-American countries.

Onion and bacon soup (France)

4 servings

100 gr (¼ lb) streaky bacon
6–8 thinly-sliced onions
1·2 litres (2 pints) water
salt, pepper
day-old French bread, lightly toasted
grated cheese, such as Gruyère or Cheddar

Fry the bacon in its own fat till the fat runs and the bacon is crisp. Put aside the bacon to fry the onions till soft in the same fat. Add the water, salt and pepper and cook over a low heat for about 30 minutes. Chop the bacon fine.

Line an oven-proof soup tureen or a large casserole with a layer of toasted bread, sprinkle generously with cheese and bacon. Repeat this process till the bread and bacon are used up. Finally add the soup. Put the tureen or casserole in a hot oven till the soup is reheated.

Chicken stock may of course be used instead of water, and some Parmesan may be mixed with the cheese.

A meal in itself, and needing only a light salad to follow.

Cream of onion and leek soup (France)

10–12 servings

450 gr (1 lb) onions, peeled and chopped
50 gr (2 oz) salt butter
4–6 leeks (white parts only), cleaned and chopped
4 large potatoes, peeled and diced
1·8 litres (3 pints) clear chicken stock
pinch of powdered nutmeg and mace
6 dl (1 pint) scalded milk
salt, pepper (to taste)
3 dl (½ pint) scalded cream
25 gr (1 oz) unsalted butter
2 well-beaten egg yolks
grated cheese, Gruyère or Cheddar

Heat the salted butter in a saucepan, preferably one which

can later go into an oven, add the onions and the leeks and cook them gently till both are soft and golden. Add the potatoes; mix these well into the mixture to ensure that they are well covered with butter. Add the stock, salt, pepper, mace and nutmeg. Cover the pan and cook for about 40 minutes, stirring from time to time. Strain the soup through a fine sieve, or purée in a blender. Return it to the saucepan, add the milk, stir this well into the soup, then add the cream. Bring this mixture carefully to the boil, stirring more or less all the time to avoid curdling. Take the pan from the heat, stir in the fresh butter and finally the yolks. Correct for seasoning and sprinkle generously with grated cheese. Let the cheese spread, then put the pan either into a very hot oven, to let the cheese brown and bubble, or under the grill.

Milk and onion soup

4 servings

6 large onions, peeled and finely chopped
100 gr (4 oz) butter
6 dl (1 pint) water
salt, pepper, sugar (to taste)
6 dl (1 pint) scalded milk
toast and grated Parmesan cheese as a garnish

Heat the butter and simmer the onions till they are lightly browned and soft. Add the water, salt, pepper and sugar, and continue cooking until the onions are very soft. Add the milk, stir well and serve hot, with toast and cheese.

This soup can be thickened slightly by whisking 2 well-beaten eggs into 1·5 dl (¼ pint) or so of cream, adding these cautiously after the milk.

Onion and tomato soup (USA)

4 servings

4 large onions
50 gr (2 oz) butter
2 cloves garlic (peeled and chopped)
a good handful of parsley
1 bay leaf
1 sprig fresh thyme
1·2 litres (2 pints) meat stock
1 tin pulped tomatoes
salt, pepper
1 teaspoonful sugar
chopped parsley, chives and French bread and Gruyère cheese as a garnish

Peel and cut the onions coarsely. Heat the butter. Add the onions, garlic, parsley, bay leaf and thyme. Cook till the onions are soft. Add the stock, bring this to the boil, lower the heat and cook the soup slowly for about 30 minutes. Discard the herbs. Add the tomatoes, cover the pan and continue cooking another 10 minutes or so. Add salt, pepper and sugar. Stir well and serve garnished with chopped parsley and chives, chunks of French bread and a bowl of grated Gruyère cheese.

Poached eggs may also be added as a garnish.

Tourrin bordelais (France)

The name of this soup, much appreciated in the south-west and Bordelais regions of France, means basically onion soup. There are several recipes, varying from district to district. In some parts of the country, i.e. the Périgord, tomatoes are added; in the Languedoc area, goose fat is used. It is often served at wedding feasts, generously flavoured with pepper.

5–6 servings

5–6 large onions, cut into thin slices
75 gr (3 oz) pork or goose fat, or other dripping
1·8 litres (3 pints) cold water
salt, pepper
3–4 egg yolks
3 dl (½ pint) warm stock

Heat the fat in a saucepan, add the onions and cook them gently, stirring often, till they are soft and evenly cooked. Add the water, salt and pepper, bring to the boil, lower the heat and simmer for 10 minutes. Beat the egg yolks, whisk these into the warm stock, add this to the soup, reheat and serve at once. Garnish with slices of very hot, dry toast. Or slices of crisply-baked French bread can be placed into each soup bowl and the hot soup poured over them.

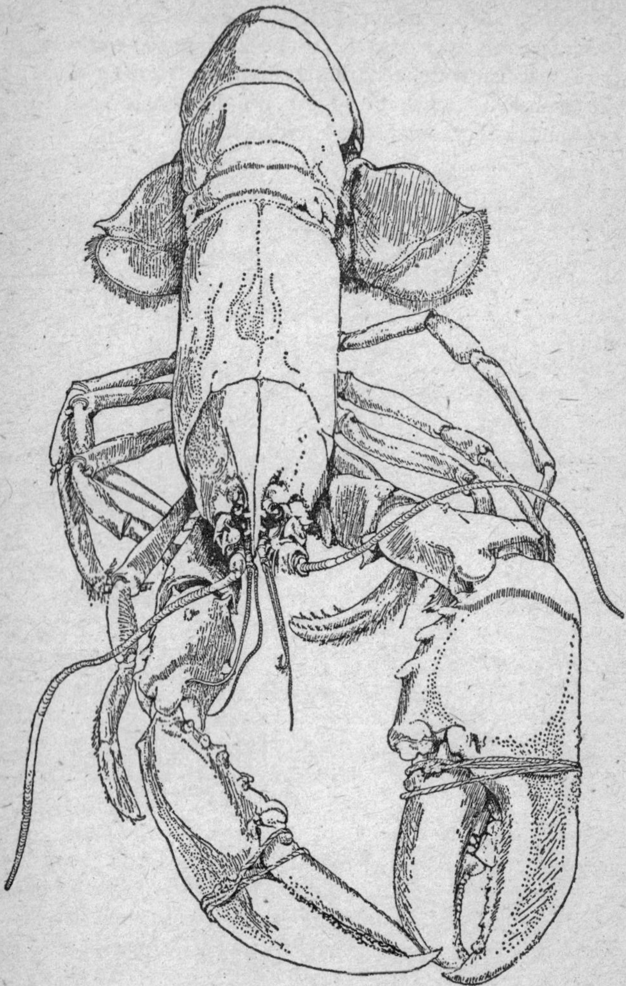

Fish soups

It is, unhappily, true to say that fish soup is the Cinderella of British soup making. Yet some of the world's most famous soups are made with fish. Those who have sampled the fish soups of the Mediterranean and the many kinds of *bisque* have found them much to their liking.

A bowl of fish soup makes a fine start to an elegant meal as well as a simple one, and many a fish soup is a meal in itself. Yet such soups are all too rarely served in British homes. Some of us attempt to make a bouillabaisse which can only be an insipid copy of the real thing. There is in any case much doubt whether the bouillabaisse is a soup at all, or really a stew.

The French, in their usual manner, have dozens of fish soups. *Bisques*, which are simply superb purées of lobster or other similar fish, are French by origin. They are easy enough to prepare, although not entirely inexpensive. No one, however, wants *bisque* every day of the week. The United States of America have their splendid New England fish chowders, and we in Britain have excellent but very neglected fish soups. Among these are mussel and eel soups and our incomparable oyster. Turtle is really a fish soup, although I have dealt with this in another chapter.

The basis of a fish soup is stock, which is easy enough to make. It consists of all the bones and trimmings, the fish heads, even skins of fish (an obliging fishmonger is willing usually to give or sell such trimmings), much of which would otherwise find its way into the dustbin. I cook my fish in a *court bouillon* and save the liquid for soups. One can poach fish in the same stock several times, by which time it only requires a few herbs or a garnish to become a subtle fish soup.

Fish stock can be clarified in the same way as meat stock. It must be cooked, skimmed of all fat and clarified with raw fish, or egg whites and shells.

To make a brown fish stock, fry the bones and trimmings before putting them into the water; but dry the bones before adding to the liquid.

For fish soups only firm, white fish should be used. Salmon, tunny, mackerel or herring would all produce an oily and unpalatable soup.

Fish stock

- 0·9–1·350 kg (2–3 lb) fish heads, trimmings of firm-fleshed fish, bones, shells of lobster, shrimps and prawns when available
- bouquet garni
- 1 stalk chopped celery
- 1–2 peeled, chopped onions (preferably spring onions)
- lemon rind (or a good squeeze of lemon juice)
- a good bunch of parsley
- 1·5 dl (¼ pint) white wine
- 2 cloves, 1 bay leaf, sprig of thyme
- 2·5 litres (4 pints) cold water
- 12 peppercorns
- salt to taste

Put all the ingredients into a saucepan, let them come to the boil, skim well and boil gently for 30 minutes. Strain. This stock can be used immediately, or kept in a refrigerator for 2–3 days. It keeps for some weeks in a deep-freeze. (It may well keep for some months, but I am judging from my own experience.) I usually poach fish in such a stock, using it several times over. By the time it is used for a soup it is then well flavoured and turns to jelly. Fish bones are not used to make a second stock. If a very clear stock is required, it can be clarified with egg whites, shells and raw fish, in precisely the same way as meat stock.

Fish bortsch (Russia)

- fish stock
- small pieces of crisply-fried filleted fish
- sour cream
- chopped dill or parsley

For each person allow 3 dl (½ pint) stock. Bring it to the boil, lower the heat, let it simmer for a short while and add the filleted fish; when these are hot, the soup is ready. Garnish with the sour cream and herbs. Dill is more usual than parsley in Russia and gives an excellent flavour. The proportions of the ingredients can be varied as desired.

Bisque (France)

It is not easy to decide whence this name is derived. In earlier times it was applied to a purée of wood pigeons, other poultry and game, but not to shellfish; other authorities declare it to be a word of Provençal origin. Today the name is always confined to a thick shellfish soup.

There has been much praise of the *bisque*. Vincent de la Chapelle quotes Dumas from his *Dictionary of Cuisine*: 'It is the most royal of dishes.' Grimod de la Reynière proclaimed it a food for princes and financiers; Brillat-Savarin observed that if a shadow of justice remained in this world, cooked crayfish would be the subject of divine worship.

Nowadays it is difficult to buy our shellfish uncooked. However, I give instructions for dealing with both the cooked and uncooked fish.

5–6 servings

1 dozen crayfish (or small crabs, or 2 lobsters)
3 filleted anchovies (or their equivalent in essence)
25 gr (1 oz) butter
1 each sliced onion and carrot
2 cloves
chopped parsley and thyme, or bouquet garni (tied)
1·2 litres (2 pints) fish stock or water
1 glass white wine
a little brandy (optional)
3 tablespoonfuls well-cooked rice
2 egg yolks
1·5 dl (¼ pint) cream
salt, pepper

When using ready-cooked crayfish (which is most likely), take out the body flesh and break off the tails. The latter are used as a garnish. Prepare the rest of the ingredients as below.

When simmering the onions, etc., add the crayfish shells, which add to the flavour of the stock, but remove these before mixing with the rice and pounded crayfish flesh.

Heat the butter, lightly brown the onion, carrot and herbs. Add anchovies, cloves, wine, brandy and liquid. Add the crayfish and cook them until they are a bright red. Let them cook in their own liquid, take from the pan and break off the tails. These, slipped from the shells, are used as a garnish. Scoop out the flesh from the bodies, pound these with the cooked rice, then with the stock, and rub all through a sieve. Return this to the pan and cook slowly for 20–30 minutes. Add (if desired) a little more wine, a small knob of butter, and stir from time to time. Just before serving, beat the yolks, whisk these into the cream, then into the soup. Add the crayfish tails, reheat, add salt and pepper and serve hot. This soup is rich, and should not be kept waiting.

Instead of pounding, a blender can be used. If using lobster, use the coral as a garnish. A garnish of chopped, hard-boiled egg yolk may also be used.

Bouillabaisse (France)

Although the bouillabaisse appears in many cooking books as a soup, it is not intended as such. In any case, to prepare the true Marseilles bouillabaisse away from the shores of the Mediterranean is a fairly useless occupation. The *rascasses*, the *hirondelles de la mer* and all the rest are only available along parts of the Mediterranean coast, and they are essential. One might well make an excellent fish stew, but not a true bouillabaisse.

The history and fame of the bouillabaisse go far back through the centuries. Every French gastronomic writer, and others as far back as Pliny, have written about and expounded his or her theory. Each has his only true, only authentic recipe, and each recipe is different. Most of these recipes, we are informed, make a Marseillais wince. I shall not add to his pain by giving a recipe, but I feel that since this is a book of soups, and since many people feel that bouillabaisse is a soup, it must at least get a mention. After all, this 'noble' dish did inspire Thackeray, who liked his food, to write a famous ballad of the bouillabaisse he ate with such relish at Terre Tavern in Paris many years ago.

Bouillabaisse – Breton style

(France)

This *is* a soup, and bears no relationship to the Provençal dish of the same name. Its quantities are strictly as required, and the soup is served either as it comes from the pot, or pushed through a sieve. It is all a matter of preference.

filleted flat fish, cut into cubes
butter
chopped spring onions, carrots and potatoes
finely-chopped parsley, chives and mint
salt, pepper
hot water or fish stock – 3 dl (½ pint) per serving

Heat the butter, add the vegetables, herbs, salt and pepper, and cook gently until the onions begin to brown. Add the fish, simmer this for a moment or so, add the liquid and cook over a moderate heat for 20 minutes or until the fish is tender. Serve with coarse brown bread or toast.

Fish chowder (USA)

6–8 servings

100 gr (4 oz) diced salt pork
25 gr (1 oz) butter
2 each chopped leeks, onions, and stick of celery
2·5 litres (4 pints) fish stock or water
salt, pepper
900 gr (2 lb) peeled and cubed potatoes
900 gr (2 lb) fresh cod or haddock, boned and cut into cubes
6 dl (1 pint) milk
3 dl (½ pint) thick cream
sherry as a flavouring

Put the pork and the butter into a large saucepan, let the fat run, then add the leeks, etc. Cook these, stirring all the time, till a golden-brown, add the stock or water and bring this to the boil. Add the potatoes, cook these for about 3 minutes, add the fish and continue cooking till this is tender. Add the milk and cook gently for another 15 minutes. Add the cream, salt and pepper to taste. Serve sprinkled with finely-chopped parsley or dill. (Instead of the cream, a thin flour and water paste may be used to thicken the soup, but it is not nearly as good.)

Clam soup

Clams are a kind of cockle to be found on the west coasts of Scotland and Ireland, in Devonshire and Cornwall, and in some parts of Wales. They figure largely in American cooking but are not much used in England. Alexis Soyer (who wrote among other culinary works *A Culinary Campaign, being historical reminiscences of the late war* – i.e. the Crimean war) wrote of cockles: 'They are much superior in flavour to oysters and, eaten raw, should be the same size, but if larger made into soup, or cooked in the same way as oysters.' When buying clams, their shells should be tightly closed. They can be opened with a knife or steamed open.

Clams should always be washed in several waters and the shells well scrubbed to remove any sand. This recipe is from Northern Ireland.

4 servings

1½ dozen clams
3 large potatoes, peeled and chopped
4 tablespoonfuls finely-chopped chives
25 gr (1 oz) butter
25 gr (1 oz) flour
6 dl (1 pint) milk

Wash and scrub the clams and put them into a saucepan with boiling water – just enough to keep them from burning. Boil for a few moments; when they open their shells, and the juice runs, take them from their shells and chop them small. Strain the liquid. Pour this back into a saucepan, add the milk and potatoes and cook until these soften. Add the clams, the butter and the chives. Cook a further 15 minutes. Mix the flour with sufficient milk or water to make a thin paste. Stir this into the soup to thicken it. Serve the soup very hot, with croûtons.

Instead of chives, onions and celery may be used. An excellent soup may be made with tinned or bottled clams.

Crabmeat soup (USA)

A soup from Georgia, meant to be made with fresh crabmeat, but it may be made with tinned crabmeat.

4–5 servings

50 gr (2 oz) butter
37 gr (1½ oz) flour
1·2 litres (2 pints) milk
salt, pepper and paprika, in generous quantities
1 small lemon, finely chopped with the skin
900 gr (2 lb) crabmeat
2 tablespoonfuls white wine

Heat the butter, stir in the flour and make a roux. Gradually add the milk stirring all the time. When thick, bring the mixture to the boil and add the lemon. Simmer for 15 minutes, then add the crabmeat, salt, pepper and paprika. When the soup is reheated, add the wine and serve the soup very hot. If the soup appears a little too thick, add more hot milk.

Cream of fish soup

4–5 servings

0·9–1·350 kg (2–3 lb) fish, some of which must be firm and white
1–2 sliced onions
1 sprig parsley and 1 bay leaf
2 tablespoonfuls tomato purée
2·5 litres (4 pints) water
3 dl (½ pint) dry white wine
salt, pepper
a little oil for frying

Fillet the fish, or at least remove as many bones as possible.

Put the fish in a fairly large pan, add water, onions, parsley and bay leaf and cook slowly till tender but still firm. Take the fish from the liquid, retain the latter and put aside some of the choicest pieces of fish to be used as a garnish. Pound the remaining fish, or purée it in a blender. Return this to the saucepan, strain in the liquid, stir well and simmer till the soup is hot. Add the tomato purée, salt, pepper and wine and blend thoroughly. Heat the oil, cut the reserved fish into cubes and fry the pieces lightly. Return these to the pan, simmer for a few minutes, then serve the soup hot, with French bread or crisply-fried bread.

The frying of the fish may be omitted and the reserved fish simply cut into cubes and returned to the soup.

Eel soup

Eel soup is a very British soup and a fine one into the bargain.

6 servings

2 medium-sized eels, cleaned and skinned
50 gr (2 oz) butter
1·8 litres (3 pints) water
bouquet garni (or sweet herbs)
1 sliced onion
peppercorns, 3 blades mace
salt
a small dinner roll
2 tablespoonfuls flour
1·5 dl (¼ pint) cream

Soak the eels in salt and water. Cut off and discard the heads and tails, skin and slice thinly. Simmer them in the butter in a saucepan – do not let them brown. After they have been simmering for 10 minutes, add the water, herbs, onion, peppercorns, mace, salt and the roll. Cook all this gently till the eels are tender. Take these out and keep hot. Strain the stock. Mix the flour into the cream, stir this into the stock, correct seasoning and bring it to the boil. Pour the stock over the eels (preferably in a soup tureen) and serve at once. Croûtons may be served with this soup.

The eels take about 1 hour to cook. It is important that the eels be very fresh – wriggling happily on the fishmonger's slab, in fact. (*Larousse* insists that they should be so fresh that they are killed at home.) Conger eel is probably the best for soups. In Jersey, Conger Eel Soup is garnished with marigold petals, and in the Netherlands parsley is used as a garnish and the soup heavily flavoured with capers.

Cream of smoked haddock soup

I fancy that this is almost the invention of my grand-daughter Charlotte and myself. She has an inordinate love of smoked haddock and it seemed to me a very good way to start her off with 'loving' soups with equal intensity. In no time at all she was also liking oyster and other expensive soups.

4–5 servings

- about 1·2 litres (2 pints) of the liquid in which you have cooked the breakfast haddock
- 225 gr (½ lb) smoked haddock, cooked and flaked
- 25 gr (1 oz) flour
- 25 gr (1 oz) butter
- salt, cayenne pepper
- paprika as a garnish

Heat the butter, stir in the flour, mix to a roux and add the liquid (preferably milk). When the mixture is thick, add the haddock, salt and pepper, cook until this is reheated, rub through a sieve, again reheat and serve hot with a little paprika sprinkled over the top to give a dash of colour. We served toasted sticks with it.

Mussel soup (France)

4–5 servings

- 450 gr (1 quart) fresh mussels
- 2 medium-sized filleted soles (plaice will do if the pocket so dictates)
- 3 small red mullets
- 2–3 fillets of turbot
- heads, bones, trimmings of the fish
- 2 each leeks and onions, finely chopped
- chervil to taste
- salt, pepper
- 1·5 dl (¼ pint) cream
- 50 gr (2 oz) butter
- 1 stalk celery and 1 sprig thyme, finely chopped

Scrape the mussels and wash them thoroughly. Put them into a large saucepan with about 2·5 litres (4 pints) of water, salt, pepper and thyme. Bring to the boil and cook till the mussels open. Take them from the pan, drain them and reserve their liquid. Take the mussels from the shells. Strain the liquid through muslin. Return this to the pan. Cook the heads, tails, bones, etc., of the fish in the mussel stock for 30 minutes. Strain and return this stock to the pan. Add the fish and cook gently till tender. Take out the fish. Heat half the butter and fry the vegetables till soft, but do not let them brown. Add freshly-ground pepper and the stock and cook the leeks, celery and onions till very soft. Rub this through a sieve. Break the cooked fish into pieces (not too small), making sure there are no bones. Put the pieces of fish into a large pan, add the mussels, stir the sieved liquid with the cream and the remainder of the butter, and pour this over the mussels. Sprinkle the soup with chervil, correct the seasoning and reheat till very hot. Serve with croûtons, fingers of crisp toast, or fried bread.

Dublin mussel soup (Eire)

4–5 servings

3 dozen mussels
1·5 dl (¼ pint) dry cider
1 chopped onion and 1 sprig parsley
2 finely-chopped leeks
1 good stalk finely-chopped celery
25 gr (1 oz) butter
25 gr (1 oz) flour
1·2 litres (2 pints) scalded milk
salt, freshly-ground black pepper, nutmeg (to taste)
1·5 dl (¼ pint) thick cream

Scrub the mussels and scrape off their beards. Put into a large pan with the cider, onion and parsley. Cover the pan and steam the mussels, shaking the pan from time to time, till the mussels open. Take them from the pan. Discard any which remain closed. Strain their liquid through cheese-cloth and keep it. Take the mussels from their shells and put them aside. Strain the stock. Heat the butter in a saucepan, add the leeks and celery and cook these till they are a golden colour. Sprinkle in the flour, stir and cook for 5 minutes. (It is important that the flour is properly cooked.) Gradually add the milk, salt, pepper and nutmeg. Cook the soup very slowly for 15 minutes. Add the stock, reheat, rub through a sieve, return the soup to the pan, slip in the mussels, add the cream, slowly reheat and serve.

Mussel soup (*Moules à la Marinière*) (France)

Although we treat this splendid dish as a soup, it usually appears in the fish section of French cookery books. The best type of mussel is the French, which is larger and less sandy than the English, which is apt to be despised by the French chefs. However, if the mussels are well cleaned and absolutely fresh, they are all good. In fact, there are few shellfish which have such a delicate and yet complex flavour as the mussel, as anyone who has eaten them well knows. I find it hard to say for how many people this dish is destined, for it depends so much on appetite (or, one might say, on greed!). A probable six is the answer.

About 6 servings

1·350 kg (6 pints) mussels
a good ½ cup dry white wine
1 scraped and chopped carrot
1 medium-sized, finely-chopped onion
1 good sprig parsley
1 bay leaf, 1 sprig thyme (or 1 teaspoonful dry thyme)
1 clove garlic
75 gr (3 oz) butter (about 3 tablespoonfuls)

Scrape the mussels and wash them thoroughly in several waters. Put them into a large pan with the wine, carrot, onion, parsley, bay leaf, thyme, garlic and butter. Cook the mussels quickly (a few minutes suffices) till they open. Discard any which have not opened. Take them from the pan and keep hot. Pour the juice of the mussels through muslin, or the finest of sieves, and add this to the liquid in which they were cooked. Take off the top shell of the mussels and return the mussels to the pan. Reheat and serve very hot. A dash of lemon may be added to the mussels at the last moment. Serve in a deep platter or a large soup tureen. The least quantity most people will eat is a dozen, but usually they tackle far more.

Cream of lobster soup (Australia)

6 servings

2 cups cooked, chopped lobster
1 large chopped onion
1 bay leaf
1 small cauliflower, washed and chopped
salt, pepper, grated nutmeg (to taste)
25 gr (1 oz) flour
6 dl (1 pint) milk
chopped parsley as a garnish

Put about 1·2 litres (2 pints) of water into a pan, add the onion, cauliflower and bay leaf. Cook for 30 minutes, then rub through a sieve. Return this to the pan and add salt, pepper and nutmeg.

Mix the flour with a little of the milk to a thin paste. Bring the soup to the boil, add the milk and flour paste, stir this until the stock thickens. Add the remaining milk and cook for 5 minutes. Add the lobster and continue to cook, without boiling, for 5 more minutes. Add the parsley just before serving. Fish stock, instead of water, will naturally give a better result.

Oyster soup (1) (Australia)

Australians can boast some of the finest oysters in the world. Two fine varieties are the Tom Ugly Point oysters and those of Bateman's Bay.

6 servings

1 dozen large shucked oysters
1·8 litres (3 pints) fish stock
25 gr (1 oz) flour
25 gr (1 oz) butter
2 teaspoonfuls anchovy essence or anchovy fillets
cayenne pepper, salt (to taste)
grated rind of 1 lemon

Pick the oysters and strain their liquid through cheese-cloth. Put the oysters and the strained liquid into a saucepan and cook over a low heat till they are on the point of coming to the boil and their edges curl. Take them out of the pan. Put aside but keep warm. Add the fish stock to the liquid and continue cooking. In another pan heat the butter, stir in the flour and cook to a white roux. Gradually add the fish stock, stirring all the while till the stock thickens. Add the anchovy, cayenne pepper and a little salt and cook for 10 minutes. Add the rind and the oysters. Stir just once, take the soup from the pan and serve hot.

Instead of 1·8 litres (3 pints) fish stock, one can use five parts of stock to one of wine. Perhaps it is extravagant these days to suggest oysters for making soup. Tinned ones, which never seem to me very good, could barely be used. Anyway, all of us can be extravagant for a special occasion. The splendour of this soup may be followed by an equally magnificent main course or, just as good, something of a contrasting simplicity. I am reminded that in Victorian cook books there are always several recipes for oyster soup, some suggesting 'take 50 oysters'. Ah, well . . .

Oyster soup (2) (USA)

4 servings

shucked oysters, 3 or 4 per person
6 dl (1 pint) milk
6 dl (1 pint) single cream
50 gr (2 oz) butter
1 teaspoonful salt
cayenne pepper (to taste)

Strain the liquid from the oysters through cheese-cloth into the top of a double boiler and bring it to the boil. In another pan scald the milk with the cream and stir in the butter, salt and pepper. Pour this into the top of the boiler. Stir well, add the oysters and cook over simmering water till the soup is hot, but not boiling. The oysters will rise to the top. Serve at once. The oysters can, if preferred, be cut into halves or quarters.

Prawn soup

6 servings

900 gr (2 lb) fresh prawns or shrimps
a few fish ends, heads, etc.
1 crushed clove garlic
bouquet garni
6 peppercorns
1 teaspoonful caraway seeds
1 each mild, chopped onion and chopped carrot
50 gr (2 oz) rice
6 dl (1 pint) milk
salt (to taste)

Wash the prawns (or shrimps) thoroughly, drop them into a pan with cold, slightly salted water, bring to the boil and continue cooking till they are scarlet. Strain from the pan and reserve the liquid. When the prawns are cool, remove the heads and tails and the dark vein. Return the shells to the pan, add the onion, carrot and fish ends, bouquet garni, peppercorns, caraway seeds and garlic and bring to the boil. Lower the heat and cook for 30 minutes to produce a fish stock. Strain.

In the meantime cook the rice in the milk, plus 3 dl (½ pint) of water or stock till very soft. Put aside about one-third of the cooked prawns to use as a garnish. Mix the remainder with the rice and purée this mixture in a blender. (With no blender, push the prawns through a *mouli* grater or sieve.) Pour the purée into a saucepan. Add the strained fish stock and, with this, dilute the purée to a *bisque* consistency; about 1·8 litres (3 pints) of stock should be required. Add salt. Serve hot, garnished with the remaining prawns. For an extra flourish, add a little white wine.

Tinned or frozen prawns may be used with a good fish stock.

Shrimp soup

4–6 servings

450 gr (1 lb) shelled and cleaned shrimps
1 small, finely-chopped mild onion
50 gr (1 oz) butter
1·2 litres (2 pints) rich milk
3 dl (½ pint) cream
salt, black pepper (to taste)
3 tablespoonfuls medium dry sherry

The shrimps should be cooked in a good fish stock, whether they are fresh or frozen, and then put through the fine blade of a grinder, or puréed in a blender. Heat the butter, add the onion and fry till it is a golden-brown. Add the shrimp paste and stir this over a moderate heat for 5 minutes. Take the pan from the fire, stir in the milk, cream, salt and pepper. Put the pan over hot water and cook for 30 minutes. It can also be cooked over a low fire protected by an asbestos sheet. Curdling must be avoided. Add the sherry just before serving.

Quarter-of-an-hour soup (*Sopa de Cuarto de Hora*) (Spain)
This is a recipe 'adopted' from Rupert Croft-Cooke. As he says, it is 'simple, showy and very satisfying'.

4 servings

1·2 litres (2 pints) clear fish stock
about 100 gr (4 oz) long grain rice
225 gr (½ lb) peeled, cooked shrimps
100 gr (4 oz) diced lean ham
2–3 hard-boiled eggs, chopped not too finely
salt, cayenne pepper

Bring the stock to the boil, add salt and pepper if required, add the rice and when this is half-way tender add the remaining ingredients. Continue cooking till the rice is soft. This is about 15–20 minutes, depending on the rice. Serve the soup hot. A garnish of finely-chopped parsley or other green herbs may be added, and a glass of fino sherry would not come amiss.

Poultry and game soups

While I am not in the least interested in any of the huntin', shootin' or fishin' pursuits, I am extremely interested in the results. I am also very conscious that hell hath no fury like the hunter whose game meets with careless results in the kitchen.

I would not want to be misunderstood when writing of game soups. I do not suggest for one second that those tender young birds, with their delicate plump flesh, should find their way into the stockpot, at least not in the first instance. I merely advocate that after they have been roasted or otherwise cooked and the finest of their flesh has been consumed, the carcass and lesser bits of flesh should be consigned to the stockpot. Also, there are those birds, so often shot well beyond the first flush of youth, which could find honour, glory and reincarnation as a subtle, sophisticated soup; and it is surely a fitting end.

For poultry, chicken, duck, goose and turkey, basically the same rules apply. Not all our birds are tender, nor for that matter have they much flavour, but boiling or steaming them will produce an excellent stock as well as a moderately tender bird. The bird can then be treated in a number of appetizing ways; and, of course, those carcasses, bones, legs, wings, feet and giblets all go towards making a splendid, delicate white stock for richer, succulent soups. It seems to me that many of us can have a pot of poultry stock most of the time without too much effort or expense.

To clarify game stock, rabbit or raw game meat is recommended. When cooking carcasses and bones a second stock, if available, can be used instead of water. If a brown game stock is required, fry the bones before adding the liquid, just as for beef stock.

When cooking a whole chicken in a stockpot, it is a sensible thing to wrap it up in a cheese-cloth, first wrung out in cold water. It keeps the bird in good shape and simplifies taking it out of the pan.

Chicken stock or broth

This may be made either from an ageing boiling fowl which, if not too ancient, can be utilized in another dish, or from the inferior parts of the bird; its wings, feet, giblets, etc. Failing an uncooked bird, use the carcass and any remaining bits of a roasted chicken. If using a carcass, use only enough water to cover it; if a whole, uncooked bird, use roughly 1·8–2·5 litres (3–4 pints); for the feet, etc., about 1·2 litres (2 pints).

Roast an uncooked bird for roughly 20 minutes before putting into cold water; this brings out its flavour and the meat makes better eating later. Put the fowl into cold water, add a little salt and no pepper; but do, if possible, add three or four slices of fresh, green ginger: it is available in Oriental stores and makes an immense difference to the flavour of the stock. When in season, I also add spring onions or leeks, an onion if it is mild; sometimes just a touch of celery (this can give too much of its flavour if not used with caution). Let the whole come gently to the boil, then simmer for 2 hours, skimming frequently. If possible, let the stock cool and chill overnight; skim off any remaining fat and use as required. If a pork bone is available, this can be added. The Chinese consider pork and chicken are interchangeable for this purpose.

Game stock

1 old pheasant or 2 old partridges
2·5–3·5 litres (4–6 pints) white stock or water
50 gr (2 oz) butter
3–4 mushrooms
1 each onion and carrot, peeled and chopped
1 stick chopped celery
salt (to taste)
12 peppercorns
bouquet garni

Draw and clean the birds (if not already prepared) and cut into pieces. Heat the butter in a saucepan, add the pieces of bird, and the vegetables, and simmer covered for about 20 minutes. Add the stock or water, let this come to the boil, lower the heat, skim well, add salt, peppercorns and the bouquet garni. Let this simmer for around 3 hours, strain well, remove all fat and set aside for use.

An excellent stock can also be made simply by using the carcass of the game and any odd bits of the flesh.

Cock-a-leekie (Scotland)

8–9 servings

It is not easy to trace the origin of this old recipe for a simple but good soup. According to one source, Mrs Beeton said it was served at the Burns Centenary at the Crystal Palace in 1859. I cannot find this reference in my earlier or later Beetons, but then poor Mrs B. was accused of saying many things. However, it could be that the recipe originates from cock-fighting days, when the defeated bird ended his days ignobly in the pot. Far more likely, it is simply the story of an old bird, past its first flush of youth and fit for nothing better than the pot. However, the recipe which I give below is Victorian and, as will be seen, specifies a *young* bird.

Many recipes include prunes – some say stoned, others unstoned; the more cautious say that prunes are optional. Henry Smith, a prolific culinary writer, snaps: 'The French like to add a few cooked prunes to this soup: why, goodness only knows.'

'Boil a young fowl in two quarters [2·5 litres] of white stock until it is tender. Take it up and put aside. Wash two bunches of fine leeks. Trim away the roots and part of the heads and cut them into one-inch lengths. Put them into the broth and add half a pound of boiled rice, a little pepper and salt. Boil for half an hour. Cut the fowl into neat joints, put it into the soup, boil up and serve very hot. The above is true Cock-a-leekie soup. The soup bearing this name is, however, as often served without fowl as with it. Time, one hour and a half. Probable cost, 3s 0d. Sufficient for eight or nine persons.'

Times have changed since this recipe was written. If a young fowl seems an extravagance, a carcass can be substituted, or you can use the giblets, feet, etc. The essential thing is to have chicken-flavoured soup. Obviously the old-fashioned soup will be the best and I am all for it.

Giblets soup

4 servings

4 sets of duck or 2 of goose giblets
2 peeled, chopped onions
1 chopped stalk celery
1·8 litres (3 pints) meat stock
10 peppercorns
bouquet garni
salt
50 gr (2 oz) butter
37 gr (1½ oz) oatmeal or flour
1 glass Madeira

Clean the giblets, put them in a saucepan, cover with cold water and bring to the boil. Discard the liquid, drain and dry the giblets and chop them. Return the giblets to the pan, add the onions, celery, stock, peppercorns and bouquet garni. Bring this mixture to the boil, skim, lower the heat and simmer gently for 2 hours, skimming often. Strain. Reserve the best bits of the giblets. Heat the butter and add the oatmeal; when blended, add the stock, bring to the boil and cook gently for another 30 minutes. Add Madeira, salt if required, and then the chopped giblets. Cook for a further 10 minutes and serve hot, garnished with croûtons.

Instead of Madeira, a dry red wine or sherry may be used. If using duck giblets, it is better to use four sets as they are much smaller than those of the goose.

Duck soup

This is an inexpensive but excellent soup since the duck has served its purpose as a main dish.

8–10 servings

- 1–2 duck carcasses, and any odd pieces of duck meat
- chopped stalks of celery (to taste)
- 2–3 peeled, coarsely-chopped onions
- 1–2 cloves garlic
- 1 bay leaf
- 2–3 peeled, coarsely-chopped carrots
- salt
- 6 peppercorns
- 1 good sprig coarsely-chopped fresh parsley
- peeled and chopped mushrooms

Put all the ingredients, except the mushrooms, into a saucepan with plenty of water; bring to the boil, lower the heat and simmer for 3 hours. Strain, cool and chill overnight in a refrigerator. Next day scrape off the fat from the soup. Pour the stock into the pan, add the mushrooms and cook these till tender. Serve the soup, very hot, flavoured with sherry or Madeira, and when in season, watercress as a garnish.

Instead of mushrooms, the soup may be garnished with small cooked turnip balls, or flavoured with white wine instead of sherry or Madeira. Alternatively the stock can be used as a basis for bortsch or a beetroot soup. Allow about 3 dl (½ pint) per serving.

Dried mushrooms may be used instead of fresh; grated Parmesan cheese, or a sauce of egg and lemon is used as a garnish. The stock may also be strained and served hot with finely-chopped parsley and thin strips of lean ham; or with chopped, cooked runner beans or peas.

Instead of wine, this soup may be flavoured with about 2 tablespoonfuls of soya sauce. Very fine Chinese vermicelli also makes a good garnish. Again, instead of any of the mentioned garnishes, put 1 raw egg yolk into each bowl of soup and pour boiling duck stock over the top.

Chicken tangerine soup

This is reputedly a soup of Chinese origin. Whether a Chinese cook would agree to this I rather doubt, but it is agreeable and unusual.

6–8 servings

1·8 litres (3 pints) clear chicken stock
3 dl (½ pint) strained tangerine juice
diced, cooked white chicken meat
3 tablespoonfuls diced bamboo shoots
3–4 thinly-sliced spring onions
some diced cooked ham
salt, and a pinch of monosodium
the sections from 1 or 2 tangerines, depending on size and free from pips and membrane
about 2 cups diced winter melon (optional)
finely-chopped pistachio nuts as a garnish

Heat the chicken stock and the juice together; when boiling, add the chicken, bamboo shoots, spring onions, cooked ham, salt and monosodium. Add the winter melon and the tangerine sections. Bring all this to the boil, serve without straining, sprinkled with pistachio nuts.

Winter melon is a pale green pumpkin with a slightly frosted look. Its flesh is white and rather inclined to be like cotton wool. It is a favourite ingredient in Chinese cooking.

Tinned tangerines may be used. Monosodium adds no flavour of its own but *brings out* flavour.

Goose soup

8 servings

This is another of my grandmotherly recipes. I confess I have not tried it out on a good fat English goose, but those we got in India were seldom fit for more than the stockpot.

When the goose is boiled, a good soup can be made from the liquid, although it is as well to boil it in a good stock rather than in water. Also put the giblets into the pan, together with 225 gr (½ lb) lean ham, 1 onion, 1 carrot and a head of lettuce. Bring it to the boil, then skim it well, lower the heat and cook gently till the goose is tender. Take out the goose and serve this with a good onion sauce. Make the giblets into a pie (how really penny-wise our grandmothers were). Strain the soup (which by this time is delicious, even with Indian geese), season it well with cayenne pepper and add either Madeira or sherry to taste. No salt should be required if ham has been used, this usually being salt enough. (The recipe does not mean the processed ham we get so often now; it means good salt country ham.) Time for cooking the goose is roughly 2 hours and should make 2·5 litres (4 pints) of soup at, so the recipe ends, 'a cost of 8d'. Prices are somewhat different today!

Pheasant soup

6–7 servings

2 pheasant carcasses
3–4 rashers bacon, diced
100 gr (4 oz) thinly-sliced calves' liver
50 gr (2 oz) butter
2·5 litres (4 pints) chicken stock
3 dl (½ pint) dry white wine
salt, pepper (preferably cayenne)
2 whole cloves
2 cloves garlic
pinch mace, nutmeg and, if possible, powdered juniper berries
bouquet garni
25 gr (1 oz) each butter and flour
1 glass dry sherry
4 tablespoonfuls cooked pilau rice, kept hot

Break up the carcasses. Heat the first quantity of butter, add the bones, bacon and liver. Cook them over a good heat till well brown, stirring almost all the while with a wooden spoon. Add the chicken stock, stir this well; add the wine, salt, pepper, cloves, garlic, mace or nutmeg, juniper and bouquet garni, and bring the soup to the boil. Skim, let the soup boil again and continue cooking for a couple of hours.

Strain the soup through a fine sieve into another saucepan. Pick off as much of the flesh from the carcass as possible, mix this with the liver and bacon and put twice through the fine blade of a food chopper to make a paste; alternatively, use a blender. Rub this through a sieve. Heat the stock. While this is reheating, put the second quantity of butter into a saucepan, add the flour, stir and cook to a brown roux. Add the liver and bacon paste, stir again, add the sherry, then gradually add the hot stock, stirring all the while. Bring it to the boil two or three times, then pour into a heated soup tureen containing the cooked rice.

Though a little heavy on the washing up, this is a splendid soup and it can be made, as can most soups, in advance. It is an elegant beginning to a good dinner, or it can make a meal in itself for those who want only a bowl of soup at night. It can be served with toasted sticks, or herb-flavoured toasted French bread (*see* page 35).

Cream of rabbit soup

6 servings

1 rabbit, whole or jointed
450 gr (1 lb) shin of beef
2 onions
bouquet garni
1 carrot
1 stalk celery
3 cloves
10 peppercorns
50 gr (2 oz) butter
50 gr (2 oz) flour
3 egg yolks
1·5 dl (¼ pint) double cream
2·5 litres (4 pints) water
salt

Wash the rabbit, put it into a large pan with the shin of beef, add the water, bring gently to the boil, then simmer for 1 hour. Remove the rabbit, strip off the best meat, chop this finely and pound in a mortar, or purée in a blender and rub through a sieve. Put this aside until required. Return the rest of the rabbit to the soup, add the bouquet garni, peppercorns, onions, carrot, celery and cloves. Bring all this slowly to the boil, again lower the heat and cook gently for a couple of hours to make a good stock. Skim and strain. Heat the butter, add the flour, stir to a roux and work in the pounded rabbit flesh. Add the stock, bring gently to a boil and simmer for 15 minutes. Beat the yolks, stir these into the cream, then into the soup. Bring almost to the boil, add salt and serve. The addition of a glass of port just before adding the egg yolks and cream is an obvious improvement.

Hare soup

6–8 servings

1 hare, skinned, cleaned and jointed
225 gr (½ lb) lean ham or bacon
100 gr (4 oz) butter
2 onions, peeled and coarsely cut
4 shallots, peeled
12 peppercorns
1 blade mace
bouquet garni
2·5 litres (4 pints) stock
50 gr (2 oz) flour
3 dl (½ pint) port wine
salt

Do not wash the hare. Dice the ham or bacon. Heat half the butter, add the ham or bacon and hare pieces and fry these to a light brown. Add the onions, shallots, peppercorns, mace and bouquet garni and finally the stock. Bring gently to the boil; lower the heat and simmer for 3 hours. Skim well during cooking. Strain.

Heat the remaining butter in another saucepan, add the flour and stir to a golden roux. Add the strained stock, stir and let it come to the boil; add wine and salt and simmer for a further 20 minutes. In the meantime strip off some of the meat from the hare, dice this and return it to the soup. Serve hot.

Venison soup

8–10 servings

1·350–1·8 kg (3–4 lb) venison
450 gr (1 lb) venison scraps
3–4 stalks celery
2–3 sprigs parsley
2 each carrots and onions
1 clove garlic
1 teaspoonful salt
3 peppercorns
3·5 litres (6 pints) water

Put all these ingredients into a large saucepan, bring to the boil, lower the heat and simmer for 3–4 hours, by which time the liquid will be reduced by two-thirds. Skim off as much fat as possible and pour the soup first through a fine sieve and then through cheese-cloth. Cool and chill. Skim off the layer of fat which will have formed on the top and return the soup to the pan. Reheat to serve.

This soup may be flavoured with sherry and garnished with croûtons.

Venison is not at all easy to come by these days – it comes from Scotland and is in season from October to March. Most of it, however, is tinned on the spot.

Turkey soup

8 servings

1 turkey carcass
2 bay leaves
bouquet garni
butter
2 tablespoonfuls flour
chopped celery (to taste)
450 gr (1 lb) chestnuts, fresh or left-overs
225 gr (½ lb) fresh mushrooms, or equivalent tinned or dried
4 tablespoonfuls Madeira
salt, pepper

Break up the carcass, strip off any remaining meat and put this aside. Put the bones into a saucepan, add about 3–3·5 litres (5–6 pints) water, the bay leaves and bouquet garni. Bring to a gentle boil, lower the heat and simmer for 3 hours. Strain. Heat the 2 tablespoonfuls of butter in the same saucepan, add the flour and stir this to a light brown roux. Gradually stir in about 2·5 litres (4 pints) of the stock and bring this to the boil, stirring most of the time. Add the celery and continue cooking for 20 minutes.

In the meantime heat 2 more tablespoonfuls of butter and sauté the mushrooms; if fresh they should be halved. Add these to the soup. Prepare the chestnuts. With a sharp knife slit the outer skins, put the chestnuts in cold water, bring to the boil and boil for 20 minutes or till the skins come off easily. Drain and, when cool enough to handle, remove both the outer and inner skins. Put the chestnuts into a pan and cook them either in stock from the turkey or in water. When they are very soft, rub them through a sieve, or mash in a potato-ricer. Add this purée to the soup. Dice the bits of turkey and drop these into the soup. Let this simmer till required (you can add any gravy or dressing which is available). Just before serving, add the Madeira, stir well and serve hot. If using chestnuts left over from stuffing, obviously all they need is to be mashed and added to the soup.

Goose can be substituted for turkey.

Allow about 3 dl (½ pint) soup per serving.

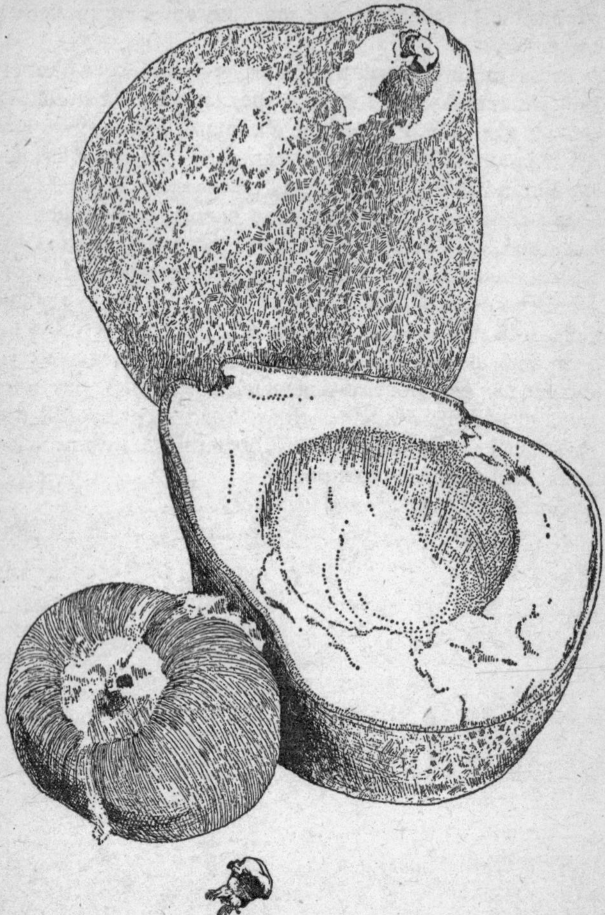

Unusual soups

On the principle that one man's meat is another man's poison, what is unusual to one is everyday to another. We might find that Ghana's aubergine and crab soup is an unusual combination, but to the Ghanaian it is a normal mixture. Usual or not, it is, I can affirm, an excellent combination, not unlike a *ratatouille* type of soup.

Some people might still consider that Birds' Nest Soup is queer, although this is fairly common nowadays with the rapid spread of Chinese eating houses. Coconut Soup is a typical West Indian soup where the coconut is as common as the wild rose in England. We might feel that avocados were meant only for salads or serving with a dressing, but to the Americans the avocado also means something with which to make delicious soups, and adding grapefruit is obvious since the two marry well.

So, all in all, it is a matter of what one is used to. It does most of us a power of good to get away from what we are used to, although I cannot pretend that one requires to be a culinary adventurer in testing the following soups. I had my guinea pigs galore and found that even the culinary 'square' approved.

Avocado soup (USA)

In Britain we are only just beginning to appreciate the flavour of the avocado pear, sometimes called *calavo* and also mistakenly *aguacate*, which seems to have been its name in Central America, its home of origin. Now it is grown in large quantities in Florida, California, South Africa and elsewhere. It is the green or purple coloured, pear-shaped fruit of the tree of the same name. When the avocado is ripe, the fruit is soft and easily pared. (*See* Iced Avocado Pear Soup, page 183.)

Usually in Britain we serve it cut into halves with a dressing. But it can be used in several ways, including the following two soups.

4 servings

2 large avocados
1·2 litres (2 pints) lightly-seasoned chicken stock
¼ teaspoonful cayenne pepper
½ cup thick cream

Cut the avocado pear into halves, if possible using a silver knife to prevent the flesh from darkening. Mash or rub it through a sieve. Add the pepper. Pour this mixture into the top of a double boiler, stir in the chicken stock and heat the soup till it boils. Add the cream, stir this till blended and reheat the soup. Serve hot, preferably with cubes of avocado.

A very bland soup. I prefer to add salt, but one must be careful not to spoil the delicate flavour of the avocado. This is a good way of using up overripe fruit.

Aubergine and crab soup (Ghana)

6–7 servings

225 gr (½ lb) stewing steak, cut into cubes
4 large aubergines, peeled and chopped
6 small onions, peeled and coarsely chopped
4 large tomatoes, peeled and chopped
flesh from 2 cooked crabs, or equivalent in tinned
1 large sweet pepper, cored and seeded
salt (to taste)
6 tablespoonfuls oil

Cook the meat till tender in 2·5 litres (4 pints) of salted water. Heat the oil and fry the onions till soft. Rub through a sieve or purée in a blender. Put aside. When the meat is tender, take from the stock and fry in the same oil till brown.

Put the tomatoes, pepper and aubergines in the meat stock. Cook till soft. Strain and rub through a sieve back into the pan. Stir this mixture thoroughly, add the onions and the meat, salt to taste, and bring again to the boil. Add the crab meat, simmer for 15 minutes and serve hot. This soup has something of the flavour of a *moussaka* or a *ratatouille*. In Ghana it is served with a *foofoo*, which is a kind of mealy paste made from the fermented root of the cassava plant. In Ghana, the quality of meat is poor. When the meat is tender it is not necessary to boil it before frying.

Birds' nest soup (Hong Kong)

The birds' nests used in this Chinese soup are not those for which small boys break their bones trying to steal eggs, but a gelatinous mass of thread spun by a type of mother sea swallow or swift in the crags and cliffs around the China coast, North Borneo, the Philippines and Indonesia. These nests, made from the dried glutinous saliva of the swallows, have a high protein value since the birds feed on small fish.

They are prised from their crevices by men who risk their lives to provide a tasty morsel for Chinese gourmets. In the circumstances it is not surprising that the cost of the nests is high. This varies (there are several varieties) and is decided by the size, shape and the number of feathers still adhering to the nests. The best ones are those with fewer feathers. Even not-so-perfect nests are highly priced. Nowadays birds' nests are often sold cleaned and prepared for the pot.

The Chinese believe that the chemical processes which take place in these birds' nests when exposed for a long time to the elements lends them a tonic value, and those who eat them are assured of good health and long life. In actual fact, birds' nests taste of nothing, the main flavour of the soup comes from the quality of the chicken stock and its garnishes.

5–6 servings

75 gr (3 oz) birds' nest (roughly) 6 nests
¼ cup water chestnuts – diced
½ cup dried Chinese mushrooms
1·8 litres (3 pints) chicken stock
1 teaspoonful salt
2 tablespoonfuls shredded ham
1 tablespoonful cornflour

Soak the mushrooms in lukewarm water for 20 minutes.

Wash the nests and soak overnight, removing the feathers with tweezers. Drain and cook the nests in water slowly for 1 hour. Drain and squeeze out all excess water and remove any remaining foreign bodies. If using the specially prepared nests, this procedure is omitted and the nests soaked for 20 minutes, drained, squeezed of excess water and then dropped into the boiling stock.

Mix the cornflour with enough water to make a thin paste. Bring the stock to the boil, add the nests, the mushrooms, chestnuts and ham. Cook gently for 15 minutes. Stir in the cornflour paste, add salt and continue cooking for 10 minutes, stirring all the time.

Instead of mushrooms and water chestnuts, hard-boiled plovers' or pigeons' eggs are added, or shredded chicken breasts, as a garnish. In Chinese restaurants in Hong Kong and Singapore I have been served – and enjoyed – whole chicken stuffed with the birds' nest, the chicken having previously been de-boned as only the Chinese know how, and served in the soup.

In Europe and America shops specializing in Chinese goods sell birds' nests in tins and these can be kept for years. Incidentally, one of my old French-cum-English cookery books recommends this soup for December eating, adds a pinch of paprika pepper, and calls the soup *Potage aux Nids d'Hirondelle.*

I have found that some Chinese dried mushrooms take up

to 30 or 40 minutes to soften. They have a distinctive flavour and are quite different from either the Polish, German or Italian dried mushrooms so easily obtainable nowadays.

Avocado and grapefruit soup (USA)

6 servings

1 large pitted avocado pear
3 dl (½ pint) each thick cream and strained grapefruit juice
salt and cayenne pepper (to taste)
1·2 litres (2 pints) almost set jellied consommé – preferably chicken

Scoop the flesh from the avocado and mash to a pulp till smooth. Stir the grapefruit juice into this and add the cream. When the mixture is blended, add salt and pepper, finally the jellied consommé. Beat this well and put into a refrigerator to set.

Serve garnished with the grapefruit sections and whipped cream. If the consommé is not sufficiently strong in itself to jell, add a little gelatine, especially in hot weather.

Chervil soup (France)

5–6 servings

2 tablespoonfuls finely-chopped fresh chervil
3 tablespoonfuls butter
2 tablespoonfuls flour
1·8 litres (3 pints) hot white stock
2 egg yolks

Heat the butter, add the flour, stir to a white roux. Gradually add the stock, and cook gently for 10 minutes, stirring all the time. Add the chervil, stir well into the soup, then take the pan from the heat. Beat the egg yolks, stir into them 2 tablespoonfuls of the hot stock, return this to the soup, stirring all the time. Reheat and serve.

Coconut soup (Bermuda)

I use my blender in making this soup – it is extremely simple. I do not think many people today can be bothered to scrape away at fresh coconut – but it grates splendidly in a blender. Having broken the coconut flesh into pieces, I put it into the blender with the coconut water. When it is all grated, squeeze it, then put it into a bowl. The resultant liquid, which must be strained, is what is called thick coconut milk. Coconut milk, frozen in a block, is now available: simply thaw this. The pulp is again covered with hot water, allowed to get cold and then squeezed. This makes the second, or thin, coconut milk. And although there is not a lot of flavour left in the pulp by now, it can be cooked with the stock to add flavour to it. Again, if using coconut milk or cream for another dish, the pulp can be cooked in fish stock, simmered for an hour, and then rubbed through a sieve. If this is then garnished with shrimps I promise a soup of excellent flavour and a good imitation of a Fijian fish and coconut soup. Allow 3 dl (½ pint) of stock per serving.

It is the brown or dried coconut which is used; for coconuts are green in their young stage, and the liquid from these is a positive nectar. The pulp, which is soft, is a divine jelly. But the brown coconuts should be full of liquid when chosen and, by shaking the coconut, you can tell if this is so. If so, it is fresh. Do not buy a cracked coconut, it will be sour.

To break a coconut, pierce the three 'eyes' or soft areas at the top of the shell – use an ice-pick or something equally sharp. Pour out the water through the holes. Revolve the nut in the hand and tap firmly with a hammer, but not too hard. The shell and the flesh come apart. Take out the flesh and cut it into small pieces and put this through the blender as recommended above.

1 coconut
6 dl (1 pint) rich stock, preferably with a hambone flavour
a little fresh thyme and a blade of mace
a few chopped shallots or spring onions
salt, pepper
2 small potatoes
3 dl (½ pint) double cream (optional)

Put the stock, thyme, mace, onions, coconut pulp and potatoes into a pot, bring to the boil, lower the heat and simmer for 20 minutes. Rub through a fine sieve. Return this to the pot. Add the coconut milk to the soup, bring this to the boil, lower the heat, stir in the cream, if using, and serve the soup hot.

The usual garnish for this kind of soup is grated toasted or dry-fried coconut, and ground nutmeg. The soup is curious, but its flavour grows on one.

If fresh coconut is impossible, a similar soup can be prepared from desiccated coconut. In this case, take 450 gr (1 lb) of the best quality desiccated coconut, put it into a basin, add 6 dl (1 pint) boiling water, let it cool, then strain or squeeze, pressing out all the liquid. Continue as with fresh coconut. Allow 3 dl (½ pint) soup per serving.

Garlic soup

An excellent number for a hot summer evening, after a small drinks party.

4 servings

6 cloves garlic
12 sweet almonds – blanched and fried quickly
2 slices diced white bread
1 good tablespoonful olive oil
0·9–1·2 litres (1½–2 pints) clear chicken stock
2 tablespoonfuls dry white wine
salt and white pepper
about 12 cubes sweet cantaloupe melon

Blend or pound the garlic and the almonds. Heat the oil, add the diced bread and the garlic paste, stir and cook till the bread cubes are a golden colour, i.e. croûtons. Take all this from the pan, pound or blend the mixture to a paste. Add the chicken stock, stir this thoroughly, add the wine, salt and pepper. Purée all this in a blender. Pour into a bowl, add the melon cubes, cool and finally chill. Serve each portion garnished with a small, pale green ice cube, but very pale, please.

Gazpacho (Spain)

5–6 servings

4 hard-boiled egg yolks (keep the whites for garnishing this or another soup)
2 tablespoonfuls olive oil
1–2 tablespoonfuls crushed garlic
1 teaspoonful dried mustard
1 large peeled and diced cucumber
2–3 cored, seeded and finely-chopped paprika peppers
2 peeled, chopped onions
1·2–1·8 litres (2–3 pints) tomato juice
juice of 1 lemon
salt and cayenne pepper
garnish:
hard-boiled egg whites, thinly-sliced lemon, croûtons and, in each plate, 2 ice cubes

Mash the yolks with the oil to a paste. Add the garlic and mustard. When completely blended, add the onions, cucumbers and peppers. Mix thoroughly, add the tomato and lemon juice, salt and pepper and chill.

For a smoother soup, purée all this in a blender. The garnish is often served in small bowls and placed on the table for all to choose from.

Gumbo (USA – New Orleans)

The history of the gumbo is part of the history of the famous Creole community of New Orleans. The urge of the *emigré* French to vary their diet, to find something to delight their taste buds, brought into being the gumbo soup – or is it a stew? During the time of the 'casket' girls who had been sent from the cities of France to become wives and cooks to expatriate Frenchmen, a Madame Langlois was asked to solve their dietary problems, which she did by bartering from neighbouring Choctaw Indians the secret of sassafras. It at once became exciting to the weary French palates.

Gumbos are based on various kinds of food and continue to be a source of culinary delight to the descendants of those Frenchmen. Most recipes insist on an ingredient called *filé*, which is derived from the tender young leaves of the sassafras tree. It is an essential of any Creole dish. Even today it is prepared and distributed by the Choctaw Indians.

There are, however, several gumbo recipes which use okra instead of *filé*, although this is considered the lazy man's gumbo. Okra is a popular vegetable in America, the Middle East, the Balkans and the Far East. It is a member of the hibiscus family and bears several names: Okra, Ladies' Fingers and Bamya are three of the more usual. I am giving a gumbo using okra and not *filé*, since *filé* is not easily obtainable in Britain.

8 servings

25 gr (1 oz) pork fat or lard
900 gr (2 lb) fresh, sliced okra
2·5 litres (4 pints) water
1 stalk celery, 1 onion, ½ green pepper, 2 cloves garlic } all finely chopped
1 small tin tomato purée
1 large bay leaf
1·350 kg (3 lb) shelled shrimps
salt, pepper

Heat the fat and fry the okra till lightly brown, crisp and no longer 'stringing'. Add the celery, garlic, onion, bay leaf, green pepper, tomato purée, salt, pepper and water. Bring to a slow boil, lower the heat and simmer for 2½ hours. Add the shrimps and continue to cook for 7 minutes slowly.

Uncooked shrimps are really meant to be used in this recipe, but it is often impossible to obtain these. Therefore use the next best. This will make a substantial soup, which can be lightened by reducing the amount of shrimps to 900 gr (2 lb).

Melon soup (Gibraltar)

4 servings

1 medium-sized sweet melon
½ teacup stale, soft breadcrumbs
2 tablespoonfuls ground almonds
1–2 crushed cloves garlic
2 tablespoonfuls olive oil
225 gr (½ lb) ice
salt, pepper

Peel and cut the melon into finger-sized pieces. Pound the breadcrumbs, garlic, almonds, salt and pepper in a mortar and gradualy add the oil. Put the ice into a soup tureen and pour over it the breadcrumb sauce. Leave till the ice melts, then add the melon. Cool, curious and quite pleasant.

If the soup should seem a little thick, dilute with iced water.

Mutton and apricot soup (Arabia)

4 servings

4 large, coarsely-chopped onions
4 large, peeled, coarsely-chopped tomatoes
1 large sprig mint
1–2 sweet peppers (red or green) cored, seeded and chopped
450 gr (1 lb) piece lamb or mutton
100 gr (4 oz) or so dried apricots
salt, pepper
1·2 litres (2 pints) cold water
about 2 tablespoonfuls fat, oil, butter or dripping

Heat the fat, add the onions, tomatoes, mint and peppers and cook till they begin to brown. Add the meat, apricots, salt, pepper and water. Bring gently to the boil, lower the heat and let the soup cook till the meat is tender. When ready, take out the meat, cut it into small pieces and return these to the pan. The soup can be made even more substantial by the addition of some cooked, chopped vermicelli.

The type of apricots used in this recipe are small, rather more dark-hued apricots than we generally see in Britain, but, if large apricots are used, it is better to cut them into halves.

If more lamb is used, this soup can be served as a *pot-au-feu*. Serve the meat, apricots and vegetables as a main course with potatoes or a plain pilau, and the soup with vermicelli or ungarnished.

Octopus soup (Mediterranean)

4 servings

- 450 gr (1 lb) octopus – cleaned, skinned and chopped
- 2 tablespoonfuls olive oil
- 1 peeled, thinly-sliced onion
- 3 peeled and seeded tomatoes
- 1·8 litres (3 pints) water or chicken stock
- salt, pepper (to taste)
- handful finely-chopped parsley
- croûtons as a garnish

Heat the oil, add the onion, let this fry and add the tomatoes. Stir this mixture well, add the octopus, the liquid, salt, pepper and parsley. Bring all this to a gentle boil, lower the heat and simmer for 3 hours. Serve hot, without straining, with the croûtons.

This soup is typically Mediterranean. I do not suppose that octopus is always to be found, even in the most adventurous fish shops in Britain, but I have seen it on rare occasions. When properly treated octopus has something of the delicate flavour of lobster.

Pomegranate soup (Iran)

Pomegranates are much used in Iran, both in sweet and savoury cooking.

8 servings

- 225 gr (½ lb) minced beef
- 1 small minced onion
- ¼ teaspoonful each pepper and ground cinnamon
- 2·5 litres (4 pints) water
- 3–4 tablespoonfuls rice
- 1 cup spinach, finely-chopped
- 1 cup parsley, finely-chopped
- ½ cup spring onion, finely-chopped
- 1 cup pomegranate juice (1 or 2 pomegranates)
- 3 tablespoonfuls sugar
- 1 tablespoonful lemon juice (optional)
- salt

Put the meat into a bowl, add the onion, a little salt, pepper and cinnamon and knead this mixture thoroughly. Break off pieces and shape into small balls. Put the water in a large pan, add 2 teaspoonfuls of salt, bring to the boil, add the rice and cook briskly for 15 minutes. Add the spinach, parsley and spring onion and cook another 15 minutes. While this is cooking, deal with the pomegranates. Cut the fruit into halves and dig out the seeds. Put these into a blender, switch on and in no time at all the juice forms. Rub this through a sieve. (Pomegranates vary enormously in size, even in those countries where they grow like weeds. A really large pomegranate will yield a good cup of juice. The kind most usual in England yield only half a cup.)

By this time the soup will be ready to take the juice. Stir this into the soup, add the sugar, stir again, then drop in the meat balls. Lower the heat and cook the soup for another 20 minutes. Just before serving, add the garnish. Taste the soup: if it seems sweet, add the lemon juice, or lime, otherwise no. The meat must be very well kneaded, to almost a rubbery texture, otherwise it will disintegrate when cooking. If in doubt, add an egg to bind the meat.

Salsify soup

This soup would not have been classed unusual 70 years ago. My Victorian cookery book lists at least 12 recipes for salsify. It is an edible root, long and spindly, which also goes by the name of oyster plant because of its peculiar flavour, not unlike that of an oyster. Indeed, the famous 'Wyvern' of the last century declares in his *Culinary Jottings for Madras*, 1878, that a purée of white salsify can be sent to the table as *bisque d'huitres*. (I am not sure of this, but in India there was a lot of pre-dinner drinking and no doubt palates were somewhat blunted by the time they reached the dining table.)

There are two types of salsify, the white and the black. The latter is usually called scorzonera. White salsify is gathered after one year's growth, scorzonera after two years. Never peel the latter before cooking, it bleeds easily and profusely. Both can be thoroughly scrubbed till they are smooth and both types take a long time to cook, at least an hour. The white variety should be cooked with vinegar to keep its colour. The following soup can be made with either type – one soup will be white, the other a rich ruby red.

4 servings

450 gr (1 lb) salsify
1·2 litres (2 pints) boiling water (flavoured with lemon if using the white salsify)
25 gr (1 oz) butter
6 peppercorns and cayenne pepper to taste
1 small onion, peeled and finely chopped
pinch of salt and celery salt
1·2 litres (2 pints) chicken or other stock
small bunch watercress (optional)
1·5–3 dl (¼–½ pint) cream
2 egg yolks

Prepare the salsify and drop them whole into boiling water. Cook for 20 minutes, add the onion, salt, celery salt, peppercorns, cayenne pepper and butter and continue cooking till the salsify is tender. Add the watercress a few minutes before the salsify is cooked. Rub this mixture through a sieve or purée in a blender. Dilute to the required consistency with the stock. Return the sieved soup to the pan and bring to the boil. Add the cream. Finally beat a little of the soup into the eggs, then stir into the pan. Again bring to a very gentle boil and serve hot.

Hungarian sauerkraut soup (*Korhely Leves*)

The translation of the Hungarian name of this soup is 'dissipated soup' and it is one of the traditional dishes served in Hungary in the early hours of the morning, after a night of dancing, drinking and gambling. It is considered as a 'pick-me-up', like the onion soup of France or the so-called 'gravy soup' of Basel.

6–8 servings

675 gr (1½ lb) sauerkraut, or 1 large tin
1 tablespoonful flour
1 tablespoonful lard or pork fat
a good flavouring of paprika
½ teaspoonful caraway seeds
1 tablespoonful finely-chopped red onion
salt (to taste)
450 gr (1 lb) Debreziner sausage, or other type of smoked sausage
water
1·5 dl (¼ pint) sour cream

Squeeze the liquid from the sauerkraut and dilute this with the water. Put it into a pan and bring to the boil. In another pan heat the fat, stir in the flour – but do not let it brown. Add the onion and fry this until soft but not brown. Add enough water to this mixture to make a thin sauce, then add the boiling diluted sauerkraut liquid. Slice the sausages, add to the stock, add the sauerkraut, salt, paprika and caraway seeds and cook steadily for at least 1 hour. Just before serving stir in the sour cream.

A meal in itself. The quantity of liquid used is entirely 'as required' – for the above quantity I would say not less than 1·8 litres (3 pints) but 2·5 litres (4) is better. If the called-for Debreziner sausages are not available, use any of the smoked sausages available nowadays in many delicatessens.

Soup with prunes (Iran)

This is a curious but pleasant soup, 'especially good for those suffering from influenza'.

100 gr (4 oz) stoned prunes
450 gr (1 lb) finely-chopped spinach
1 heaped tablespoonful finely-chopped parsley
1 large, chopped onion
100 gr (4 oz) chopped pumpkin
50 gr (2oz) rice
100 gr (2 oz) lentils
salt, pepper (to taste)
water or stock

Put all these ingredients into a pan and simmer for several hours. That is all.

The quantity of liquid varies according to how many people there are to eat the soup – it should not be too thick or too thin. Start with about 2·5 litres (4 pints) of liquid and add more if required. Allow 3 dl (½ pint) per serving.

Shark's fin soup (Hong Kong)

There are several varieties of shark's fin soup. For example, Peking prefers a rather gooey mass, while in Shanghai a thinner type is preferred; my recipe is based on the southern Chinese method. Coming as it does from Hong Kong, where everything Chinese is available, the recipe gives directions for the unprepared or completely uncooked fins. Nowadays fins are sold in the larger cities, where Chinese food is popular, in a prepared form, partially cooked, thus cutting down cooking time considerably. But whether using pre-cooked or uncooked fins, they must be well soaked.

Dishes with shark's fin are expensive almost anywhere; shark's fins are in short supply and their preparation is time-consuming. Even so, it is traditional to serve shark's fin soup at important dinners, and Chinese cooks will stake their reputations on the quality of such a soup.

6 servings

225–325 gr (8–12 oz) shark's fin
1 dessertspoonful sesame or peanut oil
1 slice spring onion
2·5-cm (1-in) piece sliced fresh ginger
2·5 litres (4 pints) chicken stock
1 tablespoonful Chinese wine or very dry sherry or gin
225 gr (8 oz) shredded chicken breast
225 gr (8 oz) shredded shrimps
2 teaspoonfuls soya sauce
1 heaped tablespoonful cornflour
flavouring:
1 dessertspoonful Chinese wine, dry sherry or gin
1 teaspoonful sesame or peanut oil
1 teaspoonful light soya sauce
pinch of salt

Wash the fins and soak them for 12 hours or till the salt has completely disappeared. Put into a pan with plenty of water and boil steadily for 3 hours, or, if still salty, change the water and reboil till the fins are completely free of salt. Drain and dry.

Heat the first quantity of oil and fry the ginger and the onion, and add the first quantity of wine. Let this simmer or soak for a few minutes, add the fins, fry these for a few minutes, add half the stock and simmer for 5 minutes. Drain and reserve the stock, much of which will have been absorbed by the fins. Mix the chicken and the shrimps with the soya sauce. Heat a little more oil in a frying pan and lightly fry the chicken and shrimps. Add the fins and when these are thoroughly reheated add all the stock and the flavouring ingredients. Mix the cornflour with enough water or stock to make a thin paste, stir this into the soup and cook it for 5 minutes.

Serve the soup hot, and put one bowl of cooked bamboo shoots on the table, another of vinegar. Each diner adds a little of the vinegar to the soup to bring out the flavour and the bamboo shoots are added as a garnish.

Sesame oil has considerably more flavour than peanut oil but, to those unused to it, it seems powerful. On the contrary, peanut oil is very bland and much employed in Chinese cooking generally.

Sour cream and dill soup (Russia)

5–6 servings

1·2 litres (2 pints) vegetable stock
4·5 dl (¾ pint) scalded sour cream
37 gr (1½ oz) flour
1 large bunch fresh dill, finely chopped
2 egg yolks
salt, pepper (to taste)
garnish of coarsely-chopped fresh dill

Heat the stock, add 3 dl (½ pint) of the sour cream, stirring all the time. Mix the flour with a little cold water to a thin paste. Stir this alternately into the soup with the remaining sour cream. When the soup is thick and smooth, add the dill, bring the soup to the boil, stirring all the while and let it boil for 2 minutes. Beat the egg yolks, add a little of the soup, beat, and return this to the soup, stirring briskly all the while. Add salt and pepper, let the soup come to the boil and add a pinch of nutmeg. Cool the soup, chill thoroughly, and serve garnished with chopped fresh dill.

The soup can also be puréed in a blender before chilling.

Walnut soup

I have a recipe for walnut soup which is attributed to Mexico, but I first 'discovered' this soup in Kashmir, staying on a houseboat. Our cook was used to cooking only 'British' food which, sadly in India, generally goes under the name of Anglo-Indian *khanna* (food) and is generally pretty nasty. But our cook, after I had convinced him that we disliked his English cooking, and more especially apple-pie made with mutton fat pastry (I cannot adequately describe the beastliness of this), produced a number of extremely good dishes, including this, which is not Kashmiri at all. Perhaps a stray Mexican finding his way into the lovely valley of flowers and walnuts gave him the recipe.

8 servings

900 gr (2 lb) walnuts (450 gr or 1 lb minus shells)
37 gr (1½ oz) butter
50 gr (2 oz) flour
salt
¼ teaspoonful chilli pepper
1·8 litres (3 pints) strained chicken stock
3 dl (½ pint) cream

Reduce the walnuts to powder. This can be done in a nut grater or similar gadget.

Heat the butter, add the flour, stir to a roux, add salt and pepper. Gradually add the chicken stock, stirring all the time, add the walnuts, lower the heat and cook gently for about 20 minutes. Add the cream, stir and serve the soup hot.

Can be garnished with pomegranate seeds, chopped chives or croûtons.

Cold white wine and vegetable soup (*Okroshka*) (Russia)
This is one of those soups where the ingredients are changed according to season, taste and availability. A soup tureen is almost a must for this soup, although a large bowl or casserole can be used instead.

5–6 servings

1 tablespoonful each dill and chives
½ tablespoonful finely-chopped parsley
4 tablespoonfuls sour cream
salt, pepper, sugar (to taste)
1 teaspoonful French mustard
1 pint shrimps
2–3 small cucumbers
6 dl (1 pint) iced chicken consommé
3 dl (½ pint) iced water
6 dl (1 pint) white wine

Put into the tureen the finely-chopped dill and chives, and the parsley, preferably European-type parsley. Add salt, pepper and sugar to taste, but not more than a teaspoonful of any. Thoroughly mix these ingredients, add the sour cream, French mustard, the small, cooked whole shrimps, 2 or 3 small cucumbers (or the equivalent in one large) peeled, thinly-sliced and previously marinated in salt and the salt squeezed out, the iced chicken consommé, white wine and iced water. Blend these ingredients together, then let the soup become very cold.

Instead of shrimps, diced mixed cold meats may be used, or a mixture of all these ingredients. It may be necessary to add more liquid to the soup: much depends on taste, or the size of the cucumbers. Sliced radishes, both white and red, are also often added, and so are sliced spring onions – beer is used instead of wine – and some Russian cooks favour the addition of sour cream or cold sliced potatoes – but these must be firm.

The cucumbers should be left in salt for an hour or so

before being added to the soup and the salt either squeezed from them or wiped off.

Cucumber and yoghourt soup (*Tarator*) (Balkans)

6 servings

1–2 peeled and diced cucumbers
salt
6 bowls each of iced yoghourt and iced water
2–3 tablespoonfuls olive oil
100 gr (4 oz) coarsely-crushed walnuts
2–3 cloves crushed garlic

Put the cucumbers into a bowl, sprinkle lightly with salt and leave for 1 hour. Stir the water into the yoghourt. Wipe the salt off the cucumber and stir the cucumber into the yoghourt. Mix the oil, walnuts and garlic to a paste. Just before serving the soup use this as a garnish in each bowl of soup.

Very refreshing, rather curious and a very typical soup of this region. *Tarator* varies from country to country but basically remains the same.

Iced yoghourt soup (Iran)

5 servings

1·2 litres (2 pints) yoghourt
a little finely-chopped fresh mint
currants or raisins as a garnish
1 cup chopped and peeled cucumber
3 dl (½ pint) iced water
salt, pepper (to taste)

Beat the yoghourt till smooth. Add salt, pepper and the mint. Stir in the water, add the cucumber, and finally a handful of either currants or raisins.

When mixed, put the soup into the refrigerator and leave till chilled.

'Welcome soup' (*Mai Hea Oe*) (Hawaii)

4 servings

½ cup chopped celery
2 tablespoonfuls butter
100 gr (¼ lb) button mushrooms, finely chopped
1 cored and finely-chopped green pepper
4 peeled, coarsely-chopped tomatoes
1 chopped clove garlic
225 gr (½ lb) fresh, chopped prawns
9 dl (1½ pints) chicken stock
2 thinly-sliced leeks, including the green part
1 dessertspoonful minced onion
1 dessertspoonful lemon juice
1 tablespoonful cornflour mixed to a paste with ½ cup water
¼ teaspoonful grated green ginger
1 bay leaf, pinch of saffron and salt to taste
garnish:
crabmeat balls

Heat the butter, sauté the celery, mushrooms, leeks, green pepper, onion and garlic. Add the tomatoes and prawns, stir, then add the remaining ingredients (except the cornflour paste), stirring well. Bring to the boil, add the cornflour, stir and cook for 5 minutes. Lower the heat, simmer the soup for 30 minutes. Take out the bay leaf and the garlic and serve the soup with crabmeat balls.

Tinned or frozen prawns may be used instead of fresh ones. The crabmeat balls can be made with fresh or tinned crabmeat (which is simpler). Instead of crabmeat balls, whole prawns can be used.

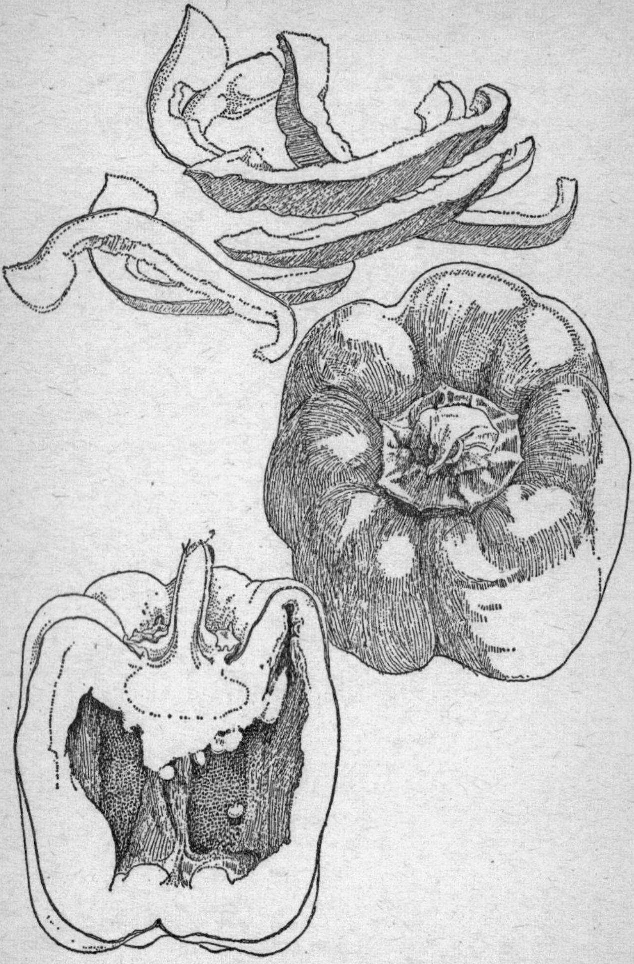

Blender soups

There is not much to say in the matter of blender or liquidizer soups. Some cooks feel that the blender reduces soups to a baby-type mush; but I do not agree with this assessment. On the contrary, I think that the blender, rightly used, has revolutionized the soup scene, and it is much used in my own kitchen.

As far as I am concerned, it offers almost limitless possibilities; mixtures are made that would otherwise be extremely difficult, i.e. in making coconut milk. In a blender it is child's play, but trying to grind it without one is not jolly at all. As far as I am concerned, it is one of the most important and essential gadgets in my kitchen.

I find that I use the word blender, which is American, rather than liquidizer; but the blender and the liquidizer are the same thing.

Almond and garlic soup (Spain)

3 servings

about ⅓ of a crustless French loaf
6 dl (1 pint) iced water
3 dl (½ pint) water or chicken soup
2 tablespoonfuls olive oil
50 gr (2 oz) blanched almonds, sautéed in oil
4 tablespoonfuls white wine
4 large peeled, chopped cloves garlic

Put all these ingredients into the blender and purée till the mixture is smooth. Rub through a fine sieve. Add another pint of iced water or enough to make a soup which is neither too thick nor too thin. Chill. When serving add an ice-cube to each portion, salt to taste and garnish with finely-chopped parsley and garlic-flavoured croûtons.

When in season, cantaloupe melon may be added to the mixture; it gives an interesting and quite distinct flavour. This soup is a variety of *gazpacho*.

Chicken and sherry soup

4 servings

- 1·2 litres (2 pints) hot chicken stock
- 4 eggs
- 1·5 dl (¼ pint) sherry
- 1 tablespoonful strained lemon juice
- salt, pepper (to taste)

Put 2 eggs, half the sherry and lemon juice into the blender. Blend for about half-a-minute at slow speed or till the mixture is well mixed and frothy. Take off the top of the blender, still operating at slow speed and gradually add half the liquid. Continue blending until all is mixed. Repeat the process with the remaining ingredients. Test for seasoning, reheat carefully and serve hot.

Gazpacho

This is basically a Spanish recipe, but has been adapted by the Americans.

4 servings

- 1·2 litres (2 pints) water
- 2 tablespoonfuls olive oil
- 1 peeled and chopped cucumber
- 2 peeled and chopped onions or equivalent in spring onions
- 1 cored, chopped green or red pepper
- 450 gr (1 lb) stale bread-crumbs – preferably dark brown
- 3–4 peeled and chopped tomatoes
- 1 tablespoonful concentrated tomato paste
- salt, cayenne pepper
- 1–3 cloves garlic, peeled and chopped

garnish:
- ice cubes
- diced tomatoes, cucumbers, finely-chopped peppers

Mix all the ingredients together (except the garnish) then purée in a blender. Pour into a bowl, add cubes and chill in a refrigerator. Serve iced. For an even smoother soup, rub the soup through a sieve after purée-ing. It is usual to serve *gazpacho* with a number of small side-dishes such as diced tomato and cucumber, and finely-chopped peppers of any colour. Spring onions will give an even finer flavour.

Cream of cheddar cheese soup (Canada)

A good soup which can be prepared in an emergency, since most of the ingredients are usually to be found in the kitchen at all times.

6 servings

a good 225 gr (½ lb) grated Cheddar cheese
25 gr (1 oz) flour
1·2 litres (2 pints) milk
50 gr (2 oz) butter
1 clove garlic
good pinch each ground nutmeg and cayenne pepper
3 dl (½ pint) white wine
2 egg yolks, lightly beaten
1·5 dl (¼ pint) cream
salt
paprika
grated Parmesan cheese

Put the cheese, flour, cayenne pepper, nutmeg and about ½ a cupful of milk into the blender and blend till the mixture is smooth. In the top of a double boiler heat the remainder of the milk, salt, butter and garlic and cook till the butter is mixed into the milk. Gradually pour the cheese mixture into the hot milk, add the wine, and heat. Mix the yolks with the cream and pour this mixture into the soup, stir and simmer for a few minutes. Serve hot, sprinkled with Parmesan cheese and a dusting of paprika.

Liver soup

6 servings

225 gr ($\frac{1}{2}$ lb) calves' liver
2 tablespoonfuls butter
6 slices crisply-toasted bread
finely-grated Parmesan cheese
finely-chopped parsley
ground cinnamon
ground nutmeg
about 2 tablespoonfuls finely-grated hazelnuts (optional)
1·8 litres (3 pints) strained beef stock
salt to taste

Chop the liver. Heat the butter and sauté the liver in this. Purée the liver with the beef stock in a blender till it is smooth. Mix with the remaining ingredients (except the toast) and bring slowly to the boil. Put a piece of toast into each soup bowl and add the soup. Alice B. Toklas calls this *Soupe à la Cardinale.*

Iced soups

I must stress iced, rather than cold, becaused iced is exactly what these soups should be. Not just cold, but well and truly chilled to bring out their subtle flavours and get full value from them.

Most of these soups are a blend of vegetables, some with stock, some with water allied with milk or cream, yoghourt or sour cream, buttermilk or thick, smooth sour milk. Add to this a dash of garlic and some fresh green herbs, and both the palate and the eye are pleased.

Chilled soups are not as new to Britain as one might think. T. R. Encherman, in his excellent book on gastronomy, *A Two Edged Sword*, records that chilled soups were introduced into England by the French aristocrats who fled to this country during the French Revolution: what a lot we owe to the French in the matter of soups.

Iced avocado pear soup (USA)

6 servings

2 ripe avocado pears
about 9 dl (1½ pints) very clear chicken stock
3 dl (½ pint) cream
salt, pepper
pinch chilli powder
garnish:
sliced avocado pear
whipped, slightly salted cream

Cut the pears into halves, take out the stone (those with green fingers can grow these into fine plants) and mash the flesh with a silver fork. Rub through a sieve. Put the avocado pulp into the top of a double boiler, stir in the stock, stirring frequently till it reaches boiling point. Add the chilli powder and the cream. Let the soup cool, then chill. Before serving, season with salt and white pepper.

Serve with a garnish – but do not use too much cream. A bland and delicious soup.

The avocado pear is sometimes erroneously called *calavo* or alligator pear. *Hobson-Jobson*, which is a glossary of Anglo-Indian terms published in 1886, lists it under alligator pear, a name which it explains is an extravagance and that *avocato* or *avogato* is a more moderate corruption of the *aguacate* or *ahuacatl* which appears to have been the local name in its homeland, Central and South America. It is, or was, also called 'Midshipman's Butter', which the authors of *Hobson-Jobson* say is suggestive of 'its merits or demerits. Had it been worth eating it would have come into the Eastern world long before'. But they also quote Grainger in 1761:

And thou green avocato, charm of sense,
Thy tipen'd marrow liberally bestows't.

While one Tom Cringle in 1830 wrote: 'The avocado with its Brobdingnag pear, as large as a purser's lantern', Joseph de Acosta, in 1608, writes that the Palta 'is a great tree and carries a faire leaf, which has a fruite like to great peares'.

Today the avocado, a great favourite in America, is becoming popular in Britain – but it seldom gets beyond being used with a so-called French dressing, or stuffed with prawns or shrimps. The fruit of a truly ripe avocado is soft and buttery and can be used in several kinds of salad.

I often watch people buying avocados and feel that a hint of how to buy one would not go amiss. Heavy, medium-sized avocados with a bright fresh appearance and fairly firm, or just beginning to soften, are usually the most delectable. After practice, one gets the feel of the fruit. If buying those which are not sufficiently soft, simply lay them aside and they will soften in time. They are easily bruised and even injured, so treat them kindly and, when cutting, do so with a silver knife.

Jellied cucumber soup

4 servings

1 large cucumber
1 very small grated onion
about ½ cup finely-chopped mint
juice of ½ lemon
1·2 litres (2 pints) partially-jellied chicken consommé
salt, pepper

Peel and grate the cucumber and remove the larger, more bothersome seeds. Add the onion, mint and lemon juice. Beat the consommé till smooth, add the cucumber mixture, continue beating till the cucumber is thoroughly integrated into the consommé; add salt and pepper, if required, and reset the soup. Serve in soup cups. Garnish with chopped chives or borage.

Iced beetroot soup (*Klodnik*)

Basically, ingredients for this famous soup, popular both in Russia and especially in Poland, are 'as to taste'. The quantities I have given are approximate.

12 servings

1·2 litres (2 pints) light, strained stock
6 dl (1 pint) fermented rye, kvass, beer, white wine, dill or beetroot pickle juice
6 dl (1 pint) sour cream or milk, strained through a cloth to become smooth
450 gr (1 lb) cooked, finely-chopped beet greens
4 tablespoonfuls finely-chopped fresh dill
a handful of finely-chopped chives and some fennel, also chopped
4–6 hard-boiled eggs, each cut into 8 pieces
1 slice cooked cold veal, diced
1 large pickled cucumber and 1 small fresh cucumber, diced
about 1½ dozen crayfish tails cut into halves (or lobster or prawn, although crayfish is classic)
1 large cooked, peeled and grated beetroot
salt, pepper
ice cubes

It is as well to start with all these ingredients cold. Mix the first ten ingredients together using, if possible, a silver tureen. When well blended, add the grated beetroot, to give the soup a pleasant pink colour. Add salt and pepper to taste, some pieces of ice (or put a piece of ice into each portion) and serve as iced or chilled as possible.

Iced parsley soup

6 servings

a really large bunch parsley
1·2 litres (2 pints) consommé, preferably chicken
3 dl (½ pint) light cream
2–3 egg yolks
salt, cayenne pepper

Wash the parsley, discard the thick stems, and chop the rest finely. Stir the chopped parsley into the stock and bring this mixture to the boil. Lower the heat, cook gently for about 25 minutes, then strain (or purée in a blender). Return the soup to the pan. Beat the egg yolks, whisk these into the cream and stir the mixture gently over a low heat into the soup. Still stirring, cook the soup till it thickens but do not let it boil. Add salt and pepper, cool and chill the soup. Serve in *bouillon* cups, garnished with a small sprig of fresh parsley and slightly salted whipped cream.

This soup, rather unexpectedly, is creamy in colour, and very rich.

Tomato and cucumber soup

5 servings

450 gr (1 lb) ripe tomatoes
1·2 litres (2 pints) clear chicken stock
25 gr (1 oz) butter
25 gr (1 oz) flour
1 small, peeled and diced cucumber
salt, pepper, pinch of nutmeg
1 teaspoonful sugar
chopped dill and parsley as a garnish
sour cream

Chop the tomatoes, put into a saucepan with half the chicken stock, and cook till the tomatoes are very soft. Either purée in a blender, or rub through a fine sieve. Heat the butter, stir in the flour, add the sieved soup and continue stirring till the mixture is smooth. Add enough of the remainder of the chicken stock to make a medium-thick soup – remember it thickens as it chills. Add salt, pepper, sugar and nutmeg. Take the pan from the heat, pour the soup into a tureen or bowl, add the cucumber and the herbs, sour cream to taste (or this may be left and served as a garnish), cool the soup then thoroughly chill. Sprinkle lightly with finely-chopped dill and/or parsley when serving.

Jellied Madrilène (USA)

3–4 servings

1½ cups tomato purée
1·2 litres (2 pints) hot beef or chicken consommé
25 gr (1 oz) gelatine

Pour the purée into a large saucepan over a good heat and cook it till it is reduced by one-third. Add the consommé. Soften the gelatine in cold water, dissolve it in warm water, then stir it into the hot soup. When it is blended, take the soup from the pan, cool and leave till set. Garnish with watercress or diced cucumber.

This soup can also be used as a filling for avocado pears.

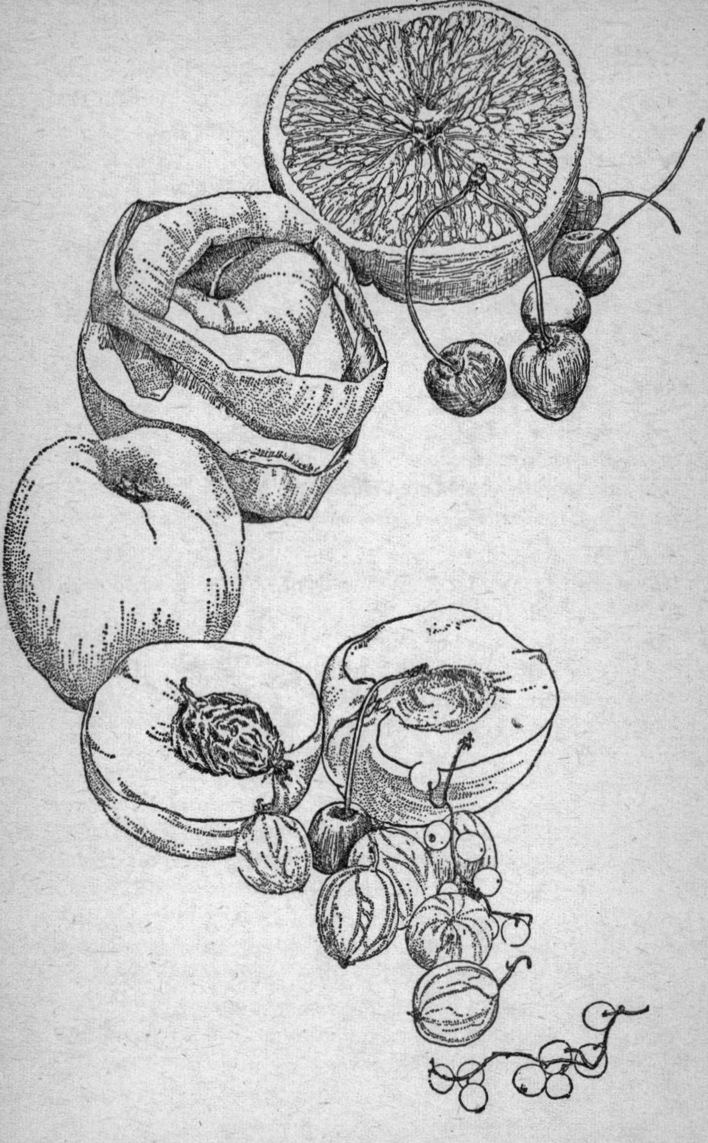

Fruit soups

It is curious how we have changed our eating habits and left out so many interesting items of diet. I first met fruit soups as a student in Germany and they came, I confess, as something of a culinary shock, although I very soon adapted myself to them and have since eaten fruit soups in many parts of the world.

And yet, one of the earliest references to fruit soups in England describes them as 'a kind of sweet pleasant broth, made rich with fruit, or vegetables and spices'. This type of soup gradually thickened until bread and rice puddings were evolved. How many of us remember that our heavy Christmas pudding started its dazzling career as a thick, heavily spiced, sweet soup?

Many of our writers from time to time have commented on the Continental fruit soups, mentioning almost with awe (and often horror) the soaked prunes which float in one of Holland's famous soups, or the iced fruit soups of Denmark, often laced with claret.

Probably no people enjoy these soups as do the Scandinavians. The Norwegians produce a soup so thick with cherries and laced with sherry it is a veritable fruit punch. The French also are extremely partial to cherry soups, while the Hungarians, ever mindful of their surfeit of luscious peaches and apricots, turn these into soups of ambrosial quality. In the Slav and Balkan countries fruit soups have been known for centuries, and no one considers them in the least strange or exotic. I feel that we in Britain could well adopt the habit of fruit soups, especially since so much of our fruit is so good and with the right amount of tartness.

Fruit soups can be served either hot or cold; at the beginning or at the end of a meal. In Brazil, where such soups have an immense vogue, they are always served at the end of a meal, an example I tend to follow, but much depends on the course of the meal. There is no doubt, however, that on a very hot day it is a good plan to round off a meal with a well-iced fruit soup to bring relief from the heat.

There are numerous garnishes with these soups; small meringues, tiny sweet *profiteroles*, sweetened croûtons; curiously enough pumpernickel, and, of course, sweet or wine biscuits. A little Cognac does not come amiss in those soups without a lacing of claret, sherry or other wine, nor does a dash of sweet liqueur. A dusting of cinnamon is also good.

The method of preparing fruit soups is simple, and the fruit can be used in single varieties or mixed, but when mixing try to get a good balance between sweet and tart. If using very sweet fruit, add a little lemon juice or peel. The usual quantity of fruit per person is between twelve ounces and one pound. I think that children could easily be encouraged to eat fruit soups, served at the end of a meal and possibly not having it stressed that they are fruit soups. These should be fairly liquid and not simply a thick purée.

Apple soup (Hungary)

4–5 servings

6 large tart apples
juice and rind of 1 lemon
a tablespoonful flour
25 gr (1 oz) butter
6 dl (1 pint) white wine
sugar (to taste)
small piece cinnamon
croûtons

Wash and chop the apples coarsely. Put into a pan with the cinnamon, lemon rind and juice and 6 dl (1 pint) water. Cook till the apples are very soft and rub through a sieve. Heat the butter, blend in the flour, gradually add the wine and one cupful of water and stir till this mixture is smooth. Add sugar to taste, stir the purée and let it all come once to the boil. Serve with croûtons, whipped cream or snow dumplings (*see* page 32).

Blackberry soup (*Kaltschale*) (Austria, Germany and Poland)

3–4 servings

900 gr (2 lb) blackberries
2–3 thin slices lemon
1·2 litres (2 pints) water
75 gr (3 oz) granulated sugar
2 cloves and 2·5 cm (1 in) piece cinnamon
iced whipped cream

Wash the fruit, pick it over and put into a saucepan with lemon, water, sugar, cinnamon and cloves. Bring slowly to the boil, lower the heat and continue cooking till the berries are soft. Reserve a few whole berries to use as a garnish. Rub the fruit through a sieve, cool and chill. Serve generously garnished with whipped cream or, just before serving, stir the cream into the soup and serve garnished with a dash of cream and whole stewed blackberries.

If liked, the soup can be slightly thickened with arrowroot, cornflour or potato flour. After the soup has been rubbed through the sieve, mix 1 dessertspoonful flour with water to a thin paste. Pour this into the soup, bring to the boil, stir and cook over a medium heat for about 5 minutes or until the soup is thick.

Apricot soup (Hungary)

3–4 servings

6–8 large ripe apricots
3 dl (½ pint) white wine or claret
1–2 strips lemon rind
6 dl (1 pint) milk
1 small bread roll
75 gr (3 oz) sugar
2 egg yolks
wine for marinating the apricots

Peel the apricots, cut them into halves and discard the stones. Put half of the apricots into the marinating wine. Put the remainder of them into the milk and add the rind and bread. Cook gently for 30 minutes and rub through a sieve. Mix this purée with the wine, add sugar and return this to the pan. Beat the egg yolks, stir these briskly into the soup, but do not let it boil. Pour this mixture over the marinating apricots and leave till cold. Serve with whipped cream as a garnish.

Cantaloupe soup (USA)

3 servings

1 large cantaloupe melon
50 gr (2 oz) butter
1 tablespoonful sugar
grated rind of 1 lemon
good pinch salt
9 dl (1½ pints) milk

Scoop out the pulp from the cantaloupe and take enough of the flesh to make a cup of diced melon. Coarsely chop the remaining melon. Heat the butter, add the melon, the sugar, lemon rind and salt and simmer this mixture for a few minutes. Add the milk, bring the mixture to the boil and continue cooking slowly for another 15 minutes. Rub the soup through a sieve or purée it in a blender, then chill it – it must be served really cold. Garnish each serving with diced melon.

When water melons are in season, use this for a garnish instead of cantaloupe.

Banana soup (1) (West Indies)

4 servings

4 large ripe bananas
1·2 litres (2 pints) cold milk
sugar and salt (to taste)
grated rind of 1 sweet orange
a little cornflour or arrowroot
Maraschino cherries as a garnish

Peel the bananas and mash them till smooth. Rub through a sieve. Gradually stir in the milk, sugar and salt. Add the orange rind, pour this mixture into a saucepan and bring to the boil. Mix the cornflour with a little water to a thin paste and pour this into the mixture. Cook till the soup becomes thick (but not too thick). Rub through a sieve. Beat vigorously just before serving and garnish with Maraschino cherries.

Banana soup (2)

Instead of milk, chicken stock may be used, but omit the sugar. I prefer the flavour of lime or lemon rind to that of orange.

Cherry soup (1) (France)

4–5 servings

25 gr (1 oz) butter
25 gr (1 oz) flour
1·8 litres (3 pints) water
900 gr (2 lb) pitted cherries
3–4 tablespoonfuls Kirsch
several crusts of bread, fried in butter

Heat the butter, add the flour, stir this to a light roux, gradually add the water and, when completely blended, add the cherries and the sugar. Bring all this to the boil, lower the heat and cook till the cherries are soft. Add the Kirsch, stir well and bring the soup to a bubbling boil. Put the fried crusts into the soup plates, add the soup while it is still bubbling, and serve at once. Escoffier flavours his cherry soup with a small piece of cinnamon and serves it with 'ladies' fingers' or *biscottes*. Other cooks favour a liqueur glass of cherry brandy as a flavouring. Sir Compton Mackenzie, in his *Third Octave*, comments on fruit soups served after the meal, and remarks that he finds this the correct place for soup of all kinds. The Chinese go one further and serve soup throughout the meal.

The flavour of this soup is very pronounced, so that anything following should be highly seasoned to hold its own.

Cherry soup (2) (Hungary)

3 servings

1·2 litres (2 pints) water
900 gr (2 lb) black, sour and pitted cherries
sugar to taste
½ teaspoonful salt
37 gr (1½ oz) flour
2 egg yolks, lightly beaten
2·5 dl (8 fl oz) thick cream, sweet or sour

Put the water into a saucepan, bring to boiling point and add the cherries, sugar and salt. Bring again to the boil, then cook slowly till the cherries are soft. Put a few aside to use as a garnish.

Mix the flour with ½ cupful of water to a smooth paste. Gradually pour this mixture into the cherry soup, stirring all the while. Bring again, with some care, to boiling point, and, still stirring, cook for 5 minutes. Take the pan from the heat. Take out about 4 tablespoonfuls of the hot soup, pour this briskly into the beaten eggs, and at once pour this mixture back into the soup. Cook for 3 minutes, stirring all the while and not allowing the soup to boil. Take from the heat and allow to get cold. Add the cream, then chill. Serve with a garnish of whole cherries.

There are excellent cherry stone pitting gadgets on the market now which can make the removing of the cherry pips simple and quick. The soup can, if preferred, be rubbed through a sieve or put into a blender to make it smoother.

Instead of sour cherries, sweet ones may be used and the sugar omitted or reduced. Also the quantity of water may be reduced and white wine added. Some cooks add a stick of cinnamon to the cherries when cooking, which is removed before serving.

This soup may also be served hot, and the reserved cherries halved for the garnish.

Peach soup (USA)

This recipe is meant for use with fresh peaches but it can be made with tinned peaches – and the sugar omitted. A recipe from the 'deep South', it is served either hot or cold, before or after a meal.

4 servings

peaches, enough to fill 2 cups when puréed
2 tablespoonfuls strained lemon juice
2 tablespoonfuls caster sugar, or to taste
1 bottle dry white wine
1 small bay leaf, 1 clove, 1 small piece cinnamon
pinch of salt

Choose very ripe peaches for this dish. Peel them. (To make peeling easy, rub the peach all over with the back of a knife, pressing it into the skin firmly, but without breaking it. The skin will peel off like the proverbial glove.) Chop and purée in a vegetable mill or blender. Put the purée into a deep bowl, sprinkle first with the lemon juice, then the sugar. Cover and leave for 20 minutes. In the meantime, bring the wine, salt and spices slowly to the boil. Simmer for a minute or so, then strain. Leave it till cold, then stir the wine into the purée. Serve, preferably chilled, but the soup may be gently heated almost to boiling point and served hot.

Cranberry soup (USA)

2 servings

450 gr (1 lb) cranberries
1 small mild onion, minced
1·8 litres (3 pints) water
37 gr (1½ oz) cornflour
1 dessertspoonful sugar
1 teaspoonful celery salt
2–3 tablespoonfuls medium dry sherry
12 gr (½ oz) butter
a little mace and marjoram
sprigs of fresh parsley as a garnish

Pick over the cranberries and cook them over a low heat till their skins burst. Press them through a sieve, adding the onion at the same time. (Or use a blender and then sieve.)

Mix the cornflour with some of the water to a thin paste. Bring the remaining water to the boil, add the cornflour, stir, and cook for 5 minutes, or till the odour of raw cornflour has disappeared. Add the sugar and celery salt, cook for 3 minutes, stir in the cranberries and add the sherry, butter, mace and marjoram. Simmer for 25 minutes. Let the soup cool, then thoroughly chill, and serve with the parsley. If using fresh marjoram and mace, remove before cooling.

Elderberry soup (Germany)

4 servings

450 gr (1 lb) elderberries
9 dl (1½ pints) boiling water
lemon peel to taste
3–4 dessertspoonfuls sago
sugar (to taste)

Pull the elderberries from their stalks, put into half the water, add the lemon peel and cook them quickly till soft. Rub through a sieve. Return the soup to the pan and add the remaining boiling water and the sago. Continue cooking till the soup is thick; add sugar just before serving.

Or use half the quantity of elderberries and add peeled and sliced apples. In this case omit the sago. Instead of lemon, the rind and juice of an orange is frequently used.

When not using sago, semolina dumplings (*see* page 32) can be used as a garnish. If the soup is too thick, it can be diluted with more water or red wine.

Orange soup

1·2 litres (2 pints) strained sweet orange juice
1 heaped dessertspoonful arrowroot
sugar (to taste)
1–2 tablespoonfuls sherry

Heat the orange juice. Mix enough water into the arrowroot to make a smooth, medium-thin paste. Pour this into the boiling juice and cook, stirring all the while, till the mixture is clear. Add sugar, take the soup from the heat, add sherry, and pour the soup into cups. Leave the soup till it is very cold, and add to each cup an ice-cube.

Rhubarb soup

3–4 servings

900 gr (2 lb) fresh young rhubarb
1·2 litres (2 pints) water
1 tablespoonful cornflour
sugar (to taste)
1·5 dl (¼ pint) thick cream
1 egg yolk

Wash the rhubarb, cut it into inch-sized pieces and pull off any 'strings'. Put the rhubarb and water into a saucepan, cook until it is very soft and add sugar. Rub through a sieve or purée in a blender. Return the soup to the pan. Mix the cornflour with water to a smooth paste. Stir this into the soup and continue cooking gently, stirring all the time, till the soup is thickened, at least 7 minutes. Beat the egg yolk, whisk it into the cream, stir this into the hot soup, take the pan from the fire and serve the soup with sweet biscuits.

Rose hip soup (English Country Recipe)

4–6 servings

4–6 oz dried rose hips
1·2 litres (2 pints) water
3 cloves
small piece cinnamon
lemon rind (to taste)
1 tablespoonful white wine
25 gr (1 oz) flour
25 gr (1 oz) butter
sugar (to taste)

Soak the rose hips till they are smooth and rounded. Boil them in the water with the rind, cloves and cinnamon. When very soft, rub through a sieve. Heat the butter, add the flour, cook this to a brown roux, and gradually add the soup. Add the wine and sugar and serve hot. Instead of wine, rum may be used.

Raspberry soup

As Raspberry and Strawberry Soup, but omit the strawberries and double the quantity of raspberries, using 6 dl (1 pint) less of water when cooking them. After thickening the soup, dilute the mixture with white wine and strained orange juice.

Raspberry and strawberry soup (1) (Continental)

4 servings

450 gr (1 lb) each raspberries and strawberries
1·8 litres (3 pints) water
sugar (to taste)
1 tablespoonful cornflour, arrowroot or potato flour

Wash and pick over the berries. Put the raspberries into a pan, add the water, bring gently to the boil, and simmer for 10 minutes. Rub them through a sieve. Purée the strawberries (without cooking) and combine them with the raspberries. Return this mixture to the pan and add sugar. Mix the cornflour with enough liquid (milk, water or a light wine) to make a thin paste. Stir this into the soup, let it come to a gentle boil, stir and cook for 5 minutes. This soup can be served hot or chilled. Wild instead of garden strawberries may be used.

Raspberry and strawberry soup (2)

Wash the fruit, rub through a sieve, add caster sugar to taste and half a bottle of white wine to each cupful of mashed fruit. Garnish with whole berries.

Strawberry soup (Balkans)

1 serving

450 gr (1 lb) strawberries (wild or garden)
sugar (to taste)
1 tablespoonful flour
2 dl ($\frac{1}{3}$ pint) water
1·5 dl ($\frac{1}{4}$ pint) claret
1·5 dl ($\frac{1}{4}$ pint) sour cream

Hull, wash and slice the strawberries. Put them into a pan and simmer till very soft. Rub through a sieve. Mix the flour with the water to make a smooth paste, add the sugar (preferably caster), claret and sour cream. Blend this into the strawberry purée and gently bring to the boil, stirring all the while. Let it boil slowly for 5 minutes, leave it to cool, then chill. Serve ice-cold, garnished with sliced strawberries and sour cream.

If sour cream is not liked, substitute sweet cream.

Fruit soup frappé (USA)

2 servings

1½ tablespoonfuls gelatine
1·5 dl (¼ pint) red wine
1·5 dl (¼ pint) each fresh raspberry and orange juice
1 tablespoonful lemon juice
1·5 dl (¼ pint) Sauternes
2 tablespoonfuls Kirsch
salt and grated nutmeg (to taste)
the segments of 1 or 2 sweet oranges, free from pips or membrane

Soften the gelatine in the red wine and dissolve it over hot water. Add the orange juice, stir this in well, add the raspberry juice, the lemon juice, Sauternes and Kirsch. Add salt and nutmeg, finally the orange segments. When the soup is cool, chill till it sets firmly. Lightly break the jelly till it resembles glistening lumps of precious stones, and serve in chilled *bouillon* cups, garnished with the thinnest possible slices of unpeeled sweet orange, dipped in caster sugar.

When fresh raspberries are not available, frozen or tinned ones may be substituted.

Mixed fresh fruit soup

2–3 servings

900 gr (2 lb) mixed fruit
75 gr (3 oz) sugar (or to taste)
a pinch of salt
2 cloves
juice of 1 lemon and some rind
about 1·2 litres (2 pints) water

Prepare the fruit, chop it coarsely and put it into a pan with the sugar, salt, cloves, water, lemon juice and rind. Bring to the boil, lower the heat and simmer till all the fruit is soft. Rub through a sieve or purée in a blender. Cool, then chill. Serve after the meal with wine biscuits.

Peaches, strawberries, pineapple, pitted and pithed oranges, rhubarb, apples and pears, all can be cooked together to make a successful soup, which should be fairly thick. It can be served with a dessertspoonful of whipped cream to each portion.

Plum soup is made in exactly the same manner and both soups may be flavoured with a generous amount of white wine. In fact, it is generally conceded that wine, either red or white, helps all fruit soups. I usually serve them rather thick, after a meal.

The Russians have an excellent apple and pear soup made in the manner of the above recipe. In Hamburg a soup is made with a mixture of raspberries, redcurrants, sweet and sour cherries and bilberries, all in equal quantities. This is thickened with cornflour, but otherwise prepared exactly as the above recipe.

Wine and beer soups

Neither wine nor beer soups are to everybody's taste, but they are interesting and extremely popular in those countries where they are served. Beer soups delight Germans especially – and some of them are curious indeed.

I remember well a beer soup which our northern German cook once served us – thick and strong, with the flavour of some German beer, the name of which mercifully escapes me. It was garnished with sweet meringues. Try as we might, it was too much for our palates, and we are eaters of almost all strange and exotic dishes. However, I do know non-Germans who delight in beer soups.

Wine soups are another matter; they are lighter, more interesting, and some are extremely good, even delicate. They are especially good for invalids seeking a change from the inevitable chicken or beef broth. Wine soups, like beer soups, are a speciality of German cooking.

Hot beer soup (Germany)

5–6 servings

1 head white cabbage
1·2 litres (2 pints) light stock – chicken, veal or vegetable
1 dessertspoonful flour
2 tablespoonfuls butter
6 dl (1 pint) hot milk
6 dl (1 pint) beer (strong ale is the best)
salt, pepper

Thoroughly wash and shred the cabbage. Heat the butter, steam the cabbage in this till it softens, stirring from time to time. Sprinkle in the flour, stir it into the cabbage, add the stock, beer, salt and pepper. Put the pan over a low flame and simmer the soup for 1 hour. Rub through a sieve, or purée in a blender. Return the soup to the pan, bring it to the boil and add the milk as soon as the soup reboils. Serve, preferably with chunks of soft brown bread, French bread or crisp toast.

Red wine soup (1)

6 servings

- 1·2 litres (2 pints) clear beef stock
- 6 dl (1 pint) dry red wine
- salt, pepper, sugar (to taste)
- ¼ teaspoonful strained lemon juice
- slices of lemon

Bring the stock to the boil and add the wine, salt, pepper, sugar and lemon juice. Serve hot, garnished with thin slices of lemon.

This soup can be served cold and jellied. Add 1 heaped tablespoonful of gelatine dissolved in cold water to the mixture, stir well, cool and chill.

Red wine soup (2)

4 servings

- 6 dl (1 pint) each red wine and water
- 3 cloves
- 2·5 cm (1 in) piece cinnamon
- 50–75 gr (2–3 oz) sugar
- thin strip orange peel
- 1 teaspoonful cornflour or potato flour

Combine the wine and water and add the spices, sugar and peel. Bring to the boil. Blend the cornflour with enough water to make a thin paste and stir into the wine. Serve with wine biscuits or sponge fingers. This soup has much the same flavour as mulled wine.

Wine soup (Germany)

3–4 servings

1 bottle dry white wine (Rhine or Moselle type)
50 gr (2 oz) butter
50 gr (2 oz) flour
grated rind and juice of 1 lemon
2 tablespoonfuls sugar
2·5 cm (1 in) piece cinnamon, or a sprinkle of ground cinnamon when serving
1 clove
3 egg yolks
3 egg whites, beaten stiffly

Bring the wine to the boil. Heat the butter and blend in the flour to make a white roux. Gradually stir in the wine, alternately with the sugar. Add the cloves and cinnamon. Stir till the soup is thick and smooth. Add the rind and the lemon juice and continue cooking and stirring for 5 minutes. Take the pan from the heat, cover it tightly and leave the soup to settle for 10 minutes.

Strain the soup and whisk in the egg yolks, one at a time, beating hard after each. It becomes light and frothy. Serve the soup in hot soup plates and float the egg white on top in a snowy drift, dusted with sifted icing sugar and lightly sprinkled with finely-grated lemon rind. Serve with wine biscuits.

The eggs may be omitted and the soup served hot, garnished simply with grated lemon rind.

Wine soup (Norway)

6 servings

1·8 litres (3 pints) water
37 gr (1½ oz) sago
37 gr (1½ oz) raisins, stoned and cleaned
2 egg yolks
sugar (to taste)
3 dl (½ pint) sweet wine
grated rind and juice of 1 lemon

Bring the water to the boil, add the sago and cook till tender. Add the raisins and cook till these are swollen. Beat the egg yolks and the sugar (at least 50 gr or 2 oz) and stir this into the soup. When blended, add the wine, lemon rind and juice. Serve hot.

Wine soup to be served as a dessert (Brazil)

4 servings
1·2 litres (2 pints) white wine
225 gr (8 oz) fine sugar
6 well-beaten egg yolks

Mix all these ingredients together and, stirring all the while, cook them gently till foamy and hot, but do not let the mixture boil. (It is best cooked in the top of a double boiler.) Serve with wine biscuits, *langues de chat* or 'ladies' fingers'.

Cold beer soup (Germany)

6 servings
1·5 litres (2½ pints) light beer
100 gr (4 oz) sugar
100 gr (4 oz) grated black bread
50 gr (2 oz) raisins
½ teaspoonful lemon-flavoured sugar
½ teaspoonful ground cinnamon

Clean the raisins and dry sauté them till they swell. Put the remaining ingredients into a tureen, add the raisins and chill. Serve very cold.

Beer soup (Poland)

4 servings
6 dl (1 pint) each beer and water
4 egg yolks
50 gr (2 oz) sugar
2 cloves
2·5 cm (1 in) piece cinnamon, or a pinch ground cinnamon
225 gr (½ lb) diced fresh white cheese
croûtons

Mix the beer and water, add the cloves and cinnamon and bring to the boil. Beat the egg yolks with the sugar and add to the soup, stirring all the while. Put the diced cheese into the soup bowls, or a soup tureen, strain the soup over the cheese and serve with croûtons.

If the cheese is not firm enough to dice, it can be creamed. Greek *fetta* cheese can be used to good effect in this kind of soup.

Wine consommé (USA)

4–5 servings

- 1·2 litres (2 pints) beef consommé
- 3 dl (½ pint) dry red wine or sherry
- salt, pepper
- lemon juice
- croûtons

Bring the consommé to the boil, and stir in the wine. Season, and add a dash of lemon juice. Serve hot, garnished with croûtons (or if preferred, lightly garnish with fresh green herbs or paprika).

Fresh food in its best season

	JAN	FEB	MARCH	APRIL	MAY	JUNE	JULY	AUG	SEPT	OCT	NOV	DEC
meat												
beef	●	●	●	●	●	●	●	●	●	●	●	●
veal		●	●	●	●	●						
spring lamb					●	●	●	●	●			
fed lamb	●	●	●	●						●	●	●
pork	●	●	●	●	●	●				●	●	●
poultry												
chicken	●	●	●	●	●	●	●	●	●	●	●	●
duck	●	●	●	●	●	●	●	●	●	●	●	●
turkey	●	●	●	●	●	●	●	●	●	●	●	●
fish												
bass	●	●	●	●	●	●	●	●	●	●	●	●
carp	●	●	●	●	●	●	●	●	●	●	●	●
cod	●	●	●	●	●	●	●	●	●	●	●	●
dab	●	●	●	●	●	●	●	●	●	●	●	●
eel	●	●	●	●	●	●	●	●	●	●	●	●
flounder	●	●	●	●	●	●	●	●	●	●	●	●
(grey) mullet	●	●	●	●	●	●	●	●	●	●	●	●
haddock	●	●	●	●	●	●	●	●	●	●	●	●
hake	●	●	●	●	●	●	●	●	●	●	●	●
halibut	●	●	●	●	●	●	●	●	●	●	●	●
herring	●	●	●	●	●	●	●	●	●	●	●	●
lemon-sole	●	●	●	●	●	●	●	●	●	●	●	●
mackerel				●	●	●	●	●	●	●	●	●
plaice	●	●	●	●	●	●	●	●	●	●	●	●

	JAN	FEB	MARCH	APRIL	MAY	JUNE	JULY	AUG	SEPT	OCT	NOV	DEC
fish continued												
pilchard	●	●	●	●	●	●	●	●	●	●	●	●
salmon	●	●	●	●	●	●	●	●	●	●	●	●
sardine				●	●	●	●	●	●	●	●	●
sole	●	●	●	●	●	●	●	●	●	●	●	●
trout	●	●	●	●	●	●	●	●	●	●	●	●
whiting				●	●	●	●	●	●	●	●	
crustaceans												
crab	●	●	●	●	●	●	●	●	●	●	●	●
lobster	●	●	●	●	●	●	●	●	●	●	●	●
prawns/shrimps	●	●	●	●	●	●	●	●	●	●	●	●
molluscs												
mussel	●	●	●	●	●	●	●	●	●	●	●	●
oyster	●	●	●	●					●	●	●	●
scallop	●	●	●	●	●	●	●	●	●	●	●	●
clam	●	●	●	●	●	●	●	●	●	●	●	●
fruit and vegetables												
anise	●									●	●	●
apple									●	●	●	
apricot						●	●					
artichoke	●	●	●	●	●						●	●
asparagus				●	●	●						
avocado	●	●	●	●	●	●	●	●	●	●	●	●
bean, lima							●	●	●	●		
bean, green			●	●	●	●	●	●				
beetroot					●	●	●	●	●	●		
blackberry							●	●				
blackcurrant							●	●				
dewberry						●						

	JAN	FEB	MARCH	APRIL	MAY	JUNE	JULY	AUG	SEPT	OCT	NOV	DEC
fruit and vegetables continued												
loganberry						●						
blueberry						●	●	●				
huckleberry						●	●	●				
broccoli	●	●	●							●	●	●
brussels sprouts	●									●	●	●
cabbage	●	●	●	●	●					●	●	●
cantaloupe						●	●	●	●			
carrot (home-grown)								●	●	●	●	
cauliflower (home-grown)									●	●	●	●
celery	●	●	●	●	●						●	●
celeriac	●	●	●								●	●
cherry					●	●	●					
collard	●	●	●								●	●
corn							●	●	●			
cranberry										●	●	●
cucumber					●	●	●	●				
currant							●					
eggplant (aubergine)							●	●	●	●		
endive and escarole								●	●	●		
gooseberry						●	●					
grapefruit (imported)	●	●	●	●						●	●	●
grapes (home-grown)								●	●	●		
kale					●	●			●	●		
leek	●	●	●	●							●	●
lettuce					●	●	●					
melon (cantaloupe)						●	●	●	●			

	JAN	FEB	MARCH	APRIL	MAY	JUNE	JULY	AUG	SEPT	OCT	NOV	DEC
fruit and vegetables continued												
mushroom	•	•	•	•					•	•	•	•
mustard greens	•	•	•									
okra							•	•	•	•		
onion, dry	•	•	•						•	•	•	•
onion, green					•	•	•	•				
orange	•	•	•	•	•							
parsley	•	•	•	•	•	•	•	•	•	•	•	•
parsnip	•	•	•							•	•	•
peach						•	•	•	•			
pear								•	•	•	•	
pea, green				•	•	•	•					
pepper							•	•	•	•		
plum						•	•	•	•			
potato	•	•	•	•	•	•	•	•	•	•	•	•
sweet potato	•								•	•	•	•
pumpkin										•		
radish			•	•	•	•	•					
raspberry						•	•	•				
redcurrant							•	•				
rhubarb			•	•	•	•						
shallot	•	•	•	•								•
spinach			•	•	•	•						
squash (marrow)									•	•	•	•
strawberry				•	•	•	•					
tangerine	•										•	•
tomato						•	•	•	•	•		
turnip and swede	•	•	•							•	•	•
watermelon						•	•	•				

Index

Theodora FitzGibbon

A Taste of Ireland £1.25

There is a flourishing Irish cookery tradition: Irish recipes are to be found tucked away in odd corners of magazines and in cookery books, but many of these recipes come from private family papers which have never before been published. They are accompanied by a remarkable series of historic photographs.

A Taste of London £1.50

The food of London is as varied as its inhabitants and its history and, Theodora FitzGibbon has mingled London's history with many excellent recipes. The superb historic photographs give a unique and touching insight into the bygone days of London.

A Taste of Scotland £1.25

The range of Scots cooking is wide, which is not surprising when one considers the influence of Scandinavia and the ancient alliance, between Scotland and France, inspiring stovies, Lorraine soup, not to mention Mary Stuart's favourite biscuits. The photographs – from between 1845 and 1900 – cast their own poignant spell.

A Taste of Wales £1.25

Here are many dishes whose Welsh names are themselves poetry: Cawl Cymreig, Brithyll â Chig Moch, Pwdin Efa, Teisen Nionod. 'Once more Theodora FitzGibbon explores the food of another country of Britain . . . authentic, historical recipes are interleaved with superb touching photographs dating from the later years of the nineteenth century' THE TIMES

A Taste of the West Country £1.25

'What a tasty dish! Dozens of them and all with regional connections . . . Somerset braised lamb, clotted cream and syllabub . . . the recipes for these and many more are presented each facing a period photograph' EXETER EXPRESS AND ECHO

The Times Cookery Book 95p
Katie Stewart

Carefully chosen from the recipes published in *The Times* over the last few years, and including many new ones, this collection of recipes by Katie Stewart is practical, varied and imaginative. Selected to suit both everyday needs and special occasions, these recipes provide a rich source of new ideas for anyone who enjoys cooking.

New Casserole Treasury 60p
Lousene Rousseau Brunner

This collection of over four hundred delicious casserole recipes comes from many countries, from great chefs and country kitchens. And the ingredients range from truffles and pâté to cabbage and beer.
Her clear, detailed and precise instructions make these dishes a joy for even the most inexperienced cook to create.

You can buy these and other Pan books from booksellers and newsagents; or direct from the following address:
Pan Books, Cavaye Place, London SW10 9PG
Send purchase price plus 15p for the first book and 5p for each additional book, to allow for postage and packing
Prices quoted are applicable in UK